BUGS
OF THE WORLD

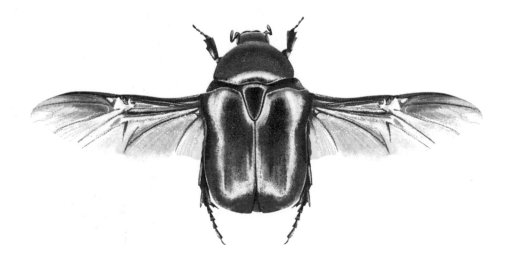

Black Dog & Leventhal Publishers
Hachette Book Group
1290 Avenue of the Americas
New York, NY 10104

www.hachettebookgroup.com
www.blackdogandleventhal.com

Originally published by NUI NUI in Italy.

First U.S. Edition: July 2020

Black Dog & Leventhal Publishers is an imprint of Running Press, a division
of Hachette Book Group. The Black Dog & Leventhal Publishers name and
logo are trademarks of Hachette Book Group, Inc.

The publisher is not responsible for websites (or their content) that are
not owned by the publisher.

The Hachette Speakers Bureau provides a wide range of authors for
speaking events. To find out more, go to www.HachetteSpeakersBureau.com
or call (866) 376-6591.

Print book interior design by Marissa Raybuck

LCCN: 2019951559

ISBNs: 978-0-7624-6896-6 (hardcover)
978-0-7624-9798-0 (ebook),
978-0-7624-6897-3 (ebook),
978-0-7624-9797-3 (ebook)

Printed in Thailand

IM

10 9 8 7 6 5 4 3 2 1

BUGS OF THE WORLD

250 CREEPY-CRAWLY CREATURES FROM AROUND PLANET EARTH

FRANCESCO TOMASINELLI
ILLUSTRATIONS BY YUMENOKAORI

BLACK DOG
& LEVENTHAL
PUBLISHERS
NEW YORK

CONTENTS

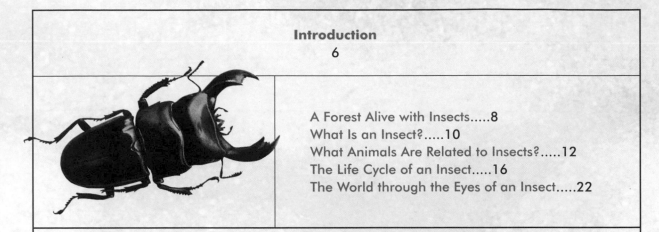

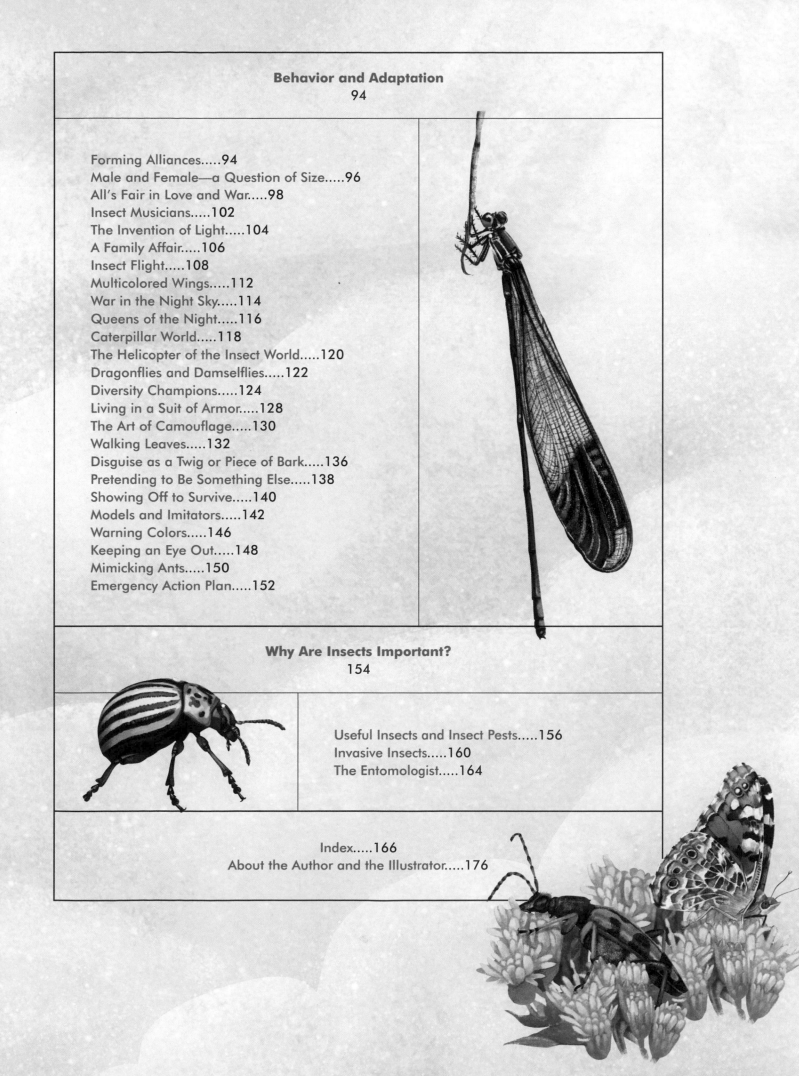

Behavior and Adaptation
94

Why Are Insects Important?
154

Insects and similar creatures can be found in all parts of Earth not completely covered in ice. They thrive in tropical forests, where the climate is warm, wet, and stable all year round. But insects have evolved so much that they are also at home in deserts and on mountaintops. They really only have trouble living in areas where human activity is too intense or the environment has become too polluted.

HOW HAVE WE CATEGORIZED THEM?

Classifying insects and other invertebrates is a very complicated process meant for specialists and scientists. In this book, we'll be describing the insects' lifestyles, the foods they eat, and their tactics in the great battle for survival. It's an exciting way to learn about the incredible diversity of appearance and behavior of these creatures.

WHAT IS A SPECIES?

Two insects belong to the same species if they can give birth to fertile offspring. In other words, they can produce young insects that can also reproduce when it's their turn. Every species is defined by a scientific name written in italics, always consisting of two words: its genus, which refers to a larger group of similar species it's a part of, and the name of the species itself. For example, the European stag beetle is known as *Lucanus cervus*.

COMMON NAME AND SCIENTIFIC NAME

There are so many insects that finding a common name for every one of them would be almost impossible. The common names you will find in this book are easy to remember, but they do not identify species very precisely and may differ from place to place, and that's why scientists prefer to use their scientific names. The stag beetle's scientific name, *Lucanus cervus*, is recognized all over the world and identifies only this particular species. Sometimes you will see the letters "sp." after the name of the genus. This means that the information applies to several or many species in that genus, rather than one specific species.

- PRAIRIE OR STEPPE

- TROPICAL FOREST

- TEMPERATE BROADLEAF FOREST

- NORTHERN CONIFER FOREST

- MEDITERRANEAN OR COASTAL VEGETATION

- SAVANNA

- DESERT

- HIGH MOUNTAIN OR TUNDRA

The great forests of Amazonia, in South America, are some of the richest environments on Earth. They are home to large mammals, such as the jaguar, and hundreds of species of birds, snakes, frogs, and lizards. But the real stars are the insects, spiders, and similar creatures. For every large animal living in these places, there are thousands of bugs, and they come in a variety of shapes, colors, and behavior patterns. Plus, they have developed all kinds of survival strategies to live in this environment.

PG 113

PG 167

PG 125

PG 126

PG 52

PG 170

PG 74

PG 166

nsects may be the strangest and most surprising group of creatures in the world, but they have a lot of things in common. They all have six legs, and as adults they always have wings, although in some cases their wings may not be visible. Finally, their bodies are divided into three distinct parts: a head with mouthparts, a thorax that supports the legs and wings, and an abdomen containing many vital organs. Insects do not have an internal skeleton like we do. Instead they have an external covering (exoskeleton) made of a substance known as chitin, which gives shape to the body.

Many beetles have impressive jaws, but they are not always used for eating. In this case, they are used as antlers to keep rival males away.

1. GIANT STAG BEETLE
(DORCUS TITANUS)

LENGTH: 4¾ in. (120 mm)

ORIGIN: Asia

Beetles have wings, but they are covered by two armor plates, known as elytrons (wing cases), that are held close to the body when the wings aren't being used.

THIS BEETLE AND THIS BUTTERFLY ARE INCREDIBLY DIFFERENT, BUT THEY ARE BOTH INSECTS.

Butterflies' heads have large eyes that they need to fly and to recognize flowers.

2

You can't see a butterfly's six legs when its wings are open. Their legs are held close to the body to help them fly.

2. MONARCH BUTTERFLY
(DANAUS PLEXIPPUS)

WINGSPAN: 4 in. (100 mm)

ORIGIN: North and Central America

Most people think spiders and centipedes are insects, but they are actually part of a larger group of animals called arthropods. Arthropods means "possessing multijointed legs." Scorpions, millipedes, and crabs are also arthropods. Like insects, they have armor-plated bodies divided into segments and different numbers of legs and antennae. Eight out of every ten animals known to scientists are arthropods. They are one of the most common forms of life on Earth. Insects, like flies and mosquitoes, are part of the arthropod group as well.

A spider's small front appendages (external body parts), known as pedipalps, are not counted as two of the animal's eight legs.

3

3. ARGIOPE SPIDER
(ARGIOPE LOBATA)

Spiders have eight legs and their bodies are divided into two distinct parts: the cephalothorax (head and thorax) and the abdomen. They belong to the very large arachnid group. Spiders are insects' greatest enemies. They are skilled predators that have invented all kinds of tactics and traps for catching their prey.

LENGTH: ¾ in. (20 mm)
ORIGIN: Europe

Rainbow crabs get their name from the bright colors of their shells.

4

4. AFRICAN RAINBOW CRAB
(CARDISOMA ARMATUM)

Crabs and crayfish are in some ways similar to scorpions, but they do not have a poisonous sting and will eat anything. They are very common in the sea, but some also live on dry land, even in forests, and return to rivers and the oceans only to lay their eggs.

WIDTH OF SHELL: 4 in. (100 mm)

ORIGIN: Africa

5. COMMON YELLOW SCORPION
(BUTHUS OCCITANUS)

Like spiders, scorpions are also arachnids. The pincers at their front end that they use to catch their prey are known as pedipalps. Their telson (tail) is armed with a poisonous sting. Like spiders, scorpions prey largely on insects, but they are less numerous than their spider cousins.

LENGTH: 4 in. (100 mm)

ORIGIN: Europe and Africa

5

The most venomous scorpions have long tails and relatively small pincers.

6. JUNGLE CENTIPEDE
(SCOLOPENDRA SUBSPINIPES)

Centipedes don't actually have 100 legs. They usually have around 40, though, which is more than enough to hunt down insects and other small animals. The first pair of legs are actually jaws, which they use to inject venom into their prey.

LENGTH: 10 in. (250 mm)
ORIGIN: Asia

Centipedes have slender antennae made up of many segments, which should not be confused with their last pair of legs.

7. GIANT MILLIPEDE
(ARCHISPIROSTREPTUS SP.)

It's also not true that millipedes have 1,000 legs. The most they can have is 750, which is still a lot! Their bodies are protected by rings of armor, and they feed on plant matter.

LENGTH: 8 in. (200 mm)
ORIGIN: Africa

Every leg on a millipede is independent of the others, but each leg's movements are coordinated with the other legs.

Insects have a fascinating life cycle. When an insect first hatches out of its egg it is known as a larva, and it looks and behaves quite differently from its adult phase. The larva spends its time eating and increasing in size before it turns into a pupa, or chrysalis, and undergoes an amazing transformation known as metamorphosis, which completely changes its appearance and way of life. The caterpillar of a butterfly is a good example of this. In some species, such as grasshoppers, the change is less obvious and the young are more or less similar to the adults, while in other species, such as dragonflies, there is no chrysalis stage at all. Each species has its own life cycle, but the better-known insects, such as ants, bees, flies, beetles, and butterflies, all undergo a complete and drastic metamorphosis.

8

The caterpillar feeds for three to four months before it is ready to change into a chrysalis.

Suspended from a twig for roughly one month in the form of a chrysalis, the caterpillar completes an amazing transformation to become a butterfly.

8. SWALLOWTAIL BUTTERFLY (PAPILIO MACHAON)

The eggs of butterflies and beetles hatch out larvae, known as caterpillars. Caterpillars are very different in appearance and ability from their adult counterpart, the butterfly. The next stage of development is the chrysalis, which is like a little tent that the insect hides in before its final transformation into an adult. The adult insect does not grow any bigger, and lives for a much shorter period of time than the larva. The main purpose of an adult insect is to reproduce.

WINGSPAN: 3¼ in. (80 mm)

ORIGIN: Europe

The wing cases of these insects are iridescent: They change color depending on the direction from which they are viewed.

The pupa completes its development while remaining motionless in the wood.

9

9. GOLDSTREIFIGER (BUPRESTIS SPLENDENS)

Some of these insects have brightly colored wing cases (the rigid shields protecting the abdomen) that can be used for making necklaces or other decorations. Larvae depend greatly on their host trees, where they spend many years at this stage.

LENGTH: 1½ in. (40 mm)

ORIGIN: Europe

⭐ **RECORD!** Goldstreifigers have the longest life cycle of any insect: They spend as many as 30 or 40 years as larvae burrowing in the wood before becoming adults.

The larva lives by burrowing deeply into the wood of a tree.

The butterfly spreads its wings and sets off on its first flight. The adult swallowtail will live for several weeks.

A newborn grasshopper is not much different from an adult.

10. DESERT LOCUST
(SCHISTOCERCA GREGARIA)

Grasshoppers and locusts pass through a number of phases as they grow. Because their armor plating does not stretch, they have to shed their skin to grow while the new covering is still soft. Grasshoppers will grow as much as one-third at each stage. Young grasshoppers are unable to fly; only adults have this ability.

LENGTH: 2¼ in. (60 mm)
ORIGIN: Africa

The adult grasshopper is a good flier, always ready to move in search of food and other members of its species.

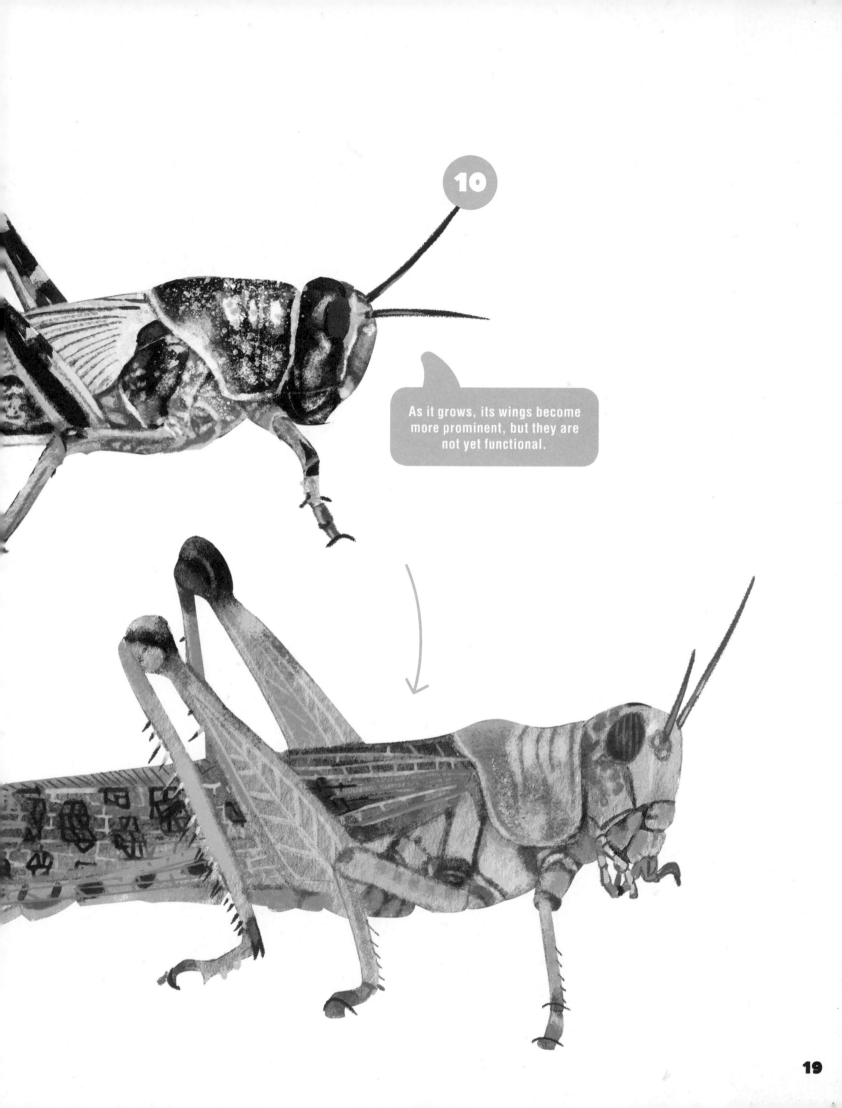

The mayfly larva lives for several months, feeding on small insects in streams and rivers.

11. MAYFLY
(EPHEMERA SP.)

One of the shortest-lived adult insects is the mayfly. Its scientific name derives from the Greek for "very brief." The larva grows in streams and rivers before metamorphosing into a small flying insect that looks like a cross between a fly and a dragonfly. The adults of some species live for only 20 or 30 minutes, just long enough to find a mate and lay their eggs.

LENGTH: ½ in. (10 mm)

ORIGIN: Europe and Asia

☆ **RECORD!** Mayflies are the shortest-lived insects: Adults of some species live for less than an hour.

The adult has no time to feed, living for just a few hours or at most for a day.

11

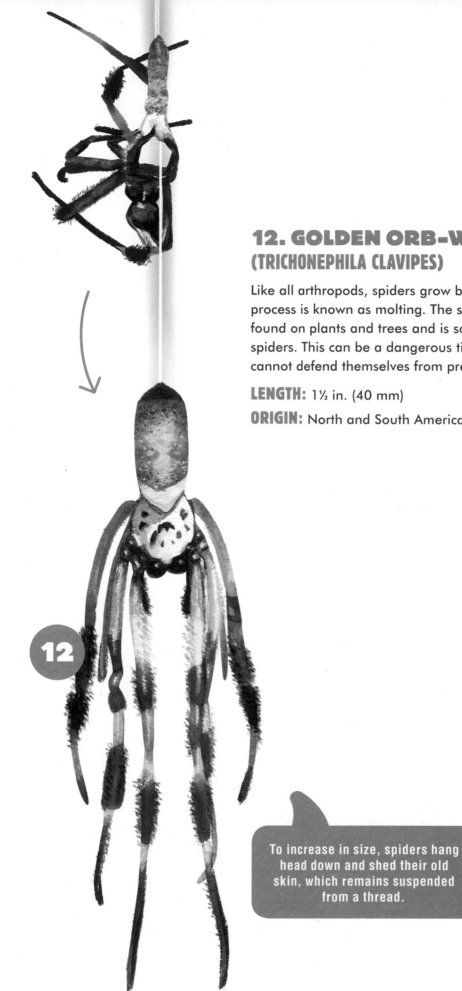

12. GOLDEN ORB-WEB SPIDER
(TRICHONEPHILA CLAVIPES)

Like all arthropods, spiders grow by shedding their skins. This process is known as molting. The skin they leave behind can be found on plants and trees and is sometimes mistaken for dead spiders. This can be a dangerous time for spiders because they cannot defend themselves from predators when they are molting.

LENGTH: 1½ in. (40 mm)

ORIGIN: North and South America

> To increase in size, spiders hang head down and shed their old skin, which remains suspended from a thread.

A wildflower meadow seen through the eyes of a pollinating insect like a bee looks very different from how a human would see it. Insects are also sensitive to ultraviolet lights, which gives them more information on the state of the flowers.

A wildflower meadow as seen by us humans.

The same meadow through the eyes of a bee, divided up into pixels and in very different colors.

13. EMPEROR DRAGONFLY
(ANAX IMPERATOR)

Insects see thanks to ommatidia, the optical units that make up their large compound eyes. Dragonflies are the most sharp-sighted of insects. Scientists believe that the image they see is a wide-angled frame divided into many "pixels," like the picture of an old-style television set.

LENGTH: 3¼ in. (80 mm)

ORIGIN: Europe and Asia

Altogether, the dragonfly's ommatidia form an image similar to what we see with our human eyes, but less well defined.

13

Every dot is an independent optical unit. A dragonfly may have 60,000 of them.

EYES

The lenses in the individual ommatidia are focused for short-distance vision, so insects can only see objects that are very close up. Since insects are so small, it's not necessary for them to see things that are more than a few yards away.

14

> Horseflies bite with a short, strong "beak" located under their heads.

14. HORSEFLY
(TABANUS SP.)

As flying insects, horseflies, which feed on the blood of mammals, need to be sharp-sighted. They have large, iridescent eyes, which change color on their angle.

LENGTH: ¾ in. (20 mm)

ORIGIN: Europe, Africa, and Asia

⭐ **RECORD!** Many horseflies have eyes with spectacular patterns, more beautiful than those of other insects.

This spider is a male, brightly colored to impress members of the other sex.

15. JUMPING SPIDER
(PHILAEUS CHRYSOPS)

Most spiders do not have good vision, but the "jumping" species are an exception. These small, sun-loving spiders locate their prey by sight, approaching sneakily like miniature cats. They are able to make out colors and recognize shapes at short distances of 16 to 20 inches (40–50 cm).

LENGTH: ½ in. (10 mm)
ORIGIN: Europe

16. GHOST CRAB
(OCYPODE SP.)

These crustaceans live on beaches in tropical countries. When threatened, they can disappear down a hole in the sand almost instantly. This is how they got their name: ghost crabs. They can react so quickly thanks in part to their highly sensitive eyes, which are similar to those of insects, but with better perception of movement and detail. They are mounted on stalks, rather like periscopes, giving them practically 360-degree vision.

WIDTH OF SHELL: 4 in. (100 mm)
ORIGIN: Africa

The eyes of the ghost crab are located on the highest part of its body so that it can see all around the beach.

PLANT EATERS (HERBIVORES)

Many insects are phytophagous, which means they only eat plant matter. Since plants are generally less nutritious than meat, they spend a large part of their lives eating and have strong jaws, beaks, or sucking devices for feeding on leaves, grass, fruits, and nectar. Every day these plant eaters consume half their body weight in plant matter and, when present in large numbers, can cause serious damage to vegetation.

Showy colors indicate that their flesh contains toxins harmful to other animals.

1. MOTH CATERPILLARS
(ARCTIIDAE FAMILY)

Caterpillars hatch from clutches of eggs and immediately devour the leaves on which they were born. Their sole concern is putting on weight before building their chrysalids and turning into adult moths or butterflies.

LENGTH: 2¼ in. (60 mm)
ORIGIN: North America

1

> Its hairy coat protects the bee fly from the cold.

2. GREATER BEE FLY
(BOMBYLIUS MAJOR)

These distant cousins of the housefly can hover in midair while feeding. They suck the nectar from flowers using a proboscis (sucking device) as long as their bodies.

LENGTH: ½ in. (8 mm)
ORIGIN: Europe

3. GREEN SHIELD BUG/STINK BUG
(PALOMENA VIRIDISSIMA)

Many species of shield bug suck chemical compounds from plants and then process and concentrate them in special glands to give them a horrible stink. These insects feed on fruit and, in large numbers, can spoil it by giving it an unpleasant taste.

LENGTH: ¾ in. (15 mm)
ORIGIN: Europe

4. NUT WEEVIL
(CURCULIO NUCUM)

The extraordinarily long "nose" of this beetle is in fact its mouth, which it uses when digging into wood and fruit.

LENGTH: ½ in. (10 mm)
ORIGIN: Europe

> Shield bugs use a kind of beak, rather like a rigid straw, to suck sap from plants and juices from fruit.

> The larva of this beetle develops inside hazelnuts.

Although they appear to be very similar, with their long hind legs adapted for jumping, crickets and grasshoppers are really different insects, both belonging to the Orthoptera order. Grasshoppers have shorter antennae and feed on plant matter.

5. SLANT-FACED GRASSHOPPER
(ACRIDA SP.)

The elongated body of this grasshopper enables it to pass itself off as a twig. The pointed head is unusual for grasshoppers, but the insect can be recognized as one by its powerful hind legs.

LENGTH: 3¼ in. (80 mm)
ORIGIN: Africa

These grasshoppers stick closely to grass stems to conceal themselves.

6. SHORT-HORNED GRASSHOPPER (PODISMA PEDESTRIS)

At high altitudes, where the weather is cold and there are strong winds, wings are not of much use. Many insects that have adapted to living in mountain environments are therefore wingless and jump instead of fly to escape predators.

LENGTH: 1¼ in. (30 mm)
ORIGIN: Europe

> Unlike most other grasshoppers, this species is wingless.

> This is a young specimen, as you can tell from its still-rudimentary wings.

7. DESERT LOCUST (SCHISTOCERCA GREGARIA)

These locusts, closely related to those shown on the following pages, have an insatiable appetite, but feed only on plants. Humans have had to contend with locusts and other similar species ever since they began growing crops. Ancient religious texts, such as the Bible and the Qur'an, speak of the damage caused by these insects.

LENGTH: 2¼ in. (60 mm)
ORIGIN: Africa

When conditions are right (rain, followed by a period of warm weather with lots of food), the migratory locusts of Africa (*Locusta migratoria*) can increase in numbers very rapidly, giving rise to giant swarms millions strong.

★ **RECORD!** Locusts form the largest insect swarms. They may consist of billions of insects and cover tens of square miles.

The adults are 2¼ inches (60 mm) in length and are good fliers and jumpers.

Locusts are continually on the move. Devouring all the plants they come across, they seriously damage farmers' crops.

Some species of cricket are not exclusively herbivores, but will eat dead animals and have strong jaws for chewing food of all kinds. However, very few are true predators like the praying mantis. Female crickets have a long swordlike ovipositor (egg-laying tube), which they use to bury their eggs underground, as well as long, slender antennae. In these respects, they differ from grasshoppers.

There are many similar species of cricket. The *Tettigonia viridissima* is one of the largest and most common in Europe.

8

8. GREAT GREEN BUSH CRICKET
(TETTIGONIA VIRIDISSIMA)

What looks like a dangerous sting on the end of this cricket's abdomen is in fact an ovipositor, an organ the female uses to inject its eggs deep into the soil.

LENGTH: 2¼ in. (60 mm)
ORIGIN: Europe

9. PREDATORY BUSH CRICKET/ SPIKED MAGICIAN
(SAGA PEDO)

Not all crickets are plant eaters. Some species, such as the larger *Saga* crickets, capture other insects with their spiny legs and devour them in the style of the praying mantis. They are some of the largest field insects, but far from common.

LENGTH: 4 in. (100 mm)
ORIGIN: Europe

9

The predatory bush cricket emerges earlier than other crickets in the spring and grows to a large size, enabling it to capture its "relatives" more easily.

10. GIANT WETA
(DEINACRIDA SP.)

Though it looks dangerous and has a sting, this enormous cricket feeds on vegetation, which it chews in its powerful jaws. It is not dangerous to humans, but it has been known to bite.

LENGTH: 4 in. (100 mm)

ORIGIN: Oceania

> With spines on its hind legs, this insect can deliver a powerful kick.

11. MOLE CRICKET
(GRYLLOTALPA GRYLLOTALPA)

No insect is better equipped than the mole cricket to dig down for tasty roots and tubers. Its powerful front legs, which are bigger and stronger than the others, are like shovels and can easily move soil aside.

LENGTH: 1½ in. (40 mm)

ORIGIN: Europe and Asia

⭐ **RECORD!** Mole crickets are the best diggers in the insect world, thanks to their powerful front legs.

> On late spring evenings, the male mole cricket comes out of its tunnel to sing. It produces a continuous trilling noise to attract suitable partners.

Dead or dying trees are an ideal growing place for the larvae of many insects, especially beetles. The larvae burrow into the tree with their strong jaws, but in many cases they take years to complete their development. If a tree is heavily infested, these insects can seriously damage it and may cause it to die.

Male capricorn beetles use their extremely long antennae to search for females in the forest.

12

12. GREAT CAPRICORN BEETLE
(CERAMBYX CERDO)

Recognizable by their spectacular long antennae, many capricorn beetles spend years in the larval stage before they become chrysalids and complete their development. As adults, they live just a few weeks, feeding on plant sap.

LENGTH: 2¼ in. (60 mm)
ORIGIN: Europe

The larva of the capricorn beetle may be up to 4 inches (10 cm) in length and is quite defenseless. As it grows, it is protected only by the thickness of the timber of its host tree.

The ovipositor is used only for reproduction. It is harmless and cannot function as a sting.

13. GIANT WOODWASP
(UROCERUS GIGAS)

This large sawfly looks like a hornet and uses its robust needlelike ovipositor to lay eggs deep in the timber of a tree, where it will hatch into a burrowing larva. The adult feeds on nectar from flowers.

LENGTH: 1½ in. (40 mm)
ORIGIN: Europe and Asia

13

14. EUROPEAN SPRUCE BARK BEETLE
(IPS TYPOGRAPHUS)

You will sometimes see curious patterns under the bark of dead trees. They are made by the larvae of beetles or weevils of the Scolytinae subfamily. The females lay their eggs in a single spot, but when the larvae emerge, they set off in different directions, carving out a strange sculpted pattern in the wood.

LENGTH: ¼ in. (5 mm)
ORIGIN: Europe and Asia

14

To see the strange patterns made by these beetles, investigate dead or dying trees. You will almost always find them in temperate forests.

The beetle grips on smooth, shiny leaves with a series of microscopic hairs.

15

15. FROG-LEGGED LEAF BEETLE
(SAGRA BUQUETI)

The males of this splendid plant-eating species with shimmering armor plating have large hind legs, which gives them their common name. These legs are not used for jumping, as you might think, but for challenging rival males. First, they raise their legs in the air and shake them. If one of them doesn't back off, they will fight. The winner is the beetle that manages to give its rival a powerful kick or plant its spiny hind legs in the rival's stomach, making it lose its balance and fall off the branch they are both on.

LENGTH: 2 in. (50 mm)

ORIGIN: Asia

From the time they first appeared on Earth in the age of dinosaurs, flowering plants have developed a close relationship with insects. Plants produce flowers rich in nectar to attract bees, flies, or butterflies. A visiting insect drinks deeply and stocks up on nectar, but at the same time, it gets covered in pollen, which it may then carry to another plant of the same species, allowing for the reproduction of that plant to take place.

This moth belongs to the hawk moth group (Sphingidae), excellent fliers that can both hover and travel at more than 25 miles per hour (40 kph). They are sometimes mistaken for hummingbirds.

16

16. MORGAN'S SPHINX MOTH
(XANTHOPAN MORGANII)

Having observed a species of white orchid that secreted its nectar deep within the flower, the famous scientist Charles Darwin, who first proposed the theory of evolution, concluded that there must be a butterfly or moth with a proboscis (sucking mouthpart) long enough to reach the bottom. The insect, the Morgan's sphinx moth, was in fact discovered after his death.

WINGSPAN: 4¾ in (120 mm)

ORIGIN: Africa

✪ **RECORD!** This moth's proboscis is possibly the longest in the world in proportion to the size of its body.

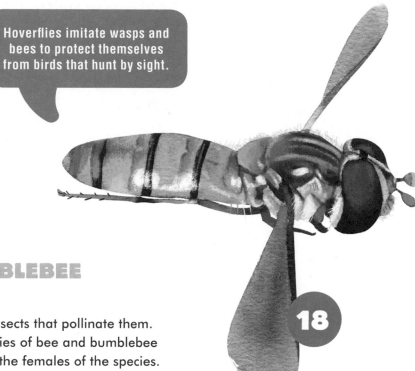

Hoverflies imitate wasps and bees to protect themselves from birds that hunt by sight.

17. RED-TAILED BUMBLEBEE (BOMBUS LAPIDARIUS)

Some species of orchid deceive the insects that pollinate them. They attract the males of certain species of bee and bumblebee by mimicking the shape and scent of the females of the species. The plant thus gets itself pollinated by the roving male, but the insect gets nothing in return.

LENGTH: ½ in. (10 mm)

ORIGIN: Europe

⭐ **RECORD!** Bumblebees are the world's hairiest insects, a characteristic that protects them from the cold.

18. HOVERFLY (SPHAEROPHORIA SP.)

These small insects of the Syrphidae family are the real champions of flight. Flapping their wings at more than 100 beats per second, they are able to hover in midair and accelerate away in a flash. To feed, however, they settle on flowers to sip nectar.

LENGTH: 3¼ in. (80 mm)

ORIGIN: Europe and Asia

Like bees, bumblebees, too, are capable of stinging. The stinger is located at the end of the abdomen, hidden in the insect's body hair.

19

19. PAINTED LADY
(VANESSA CARDUI)

Butterflies are some of the most hardworking pollinators of flowers, which they visit on fine sunny days, sucking the nectar through a long proboscis. In the course of a day, a single butterfly may visit 100 or more flowers.

WINGSPAN: 3¼ in. (80 mm)
ORIGIN: Europe and Asia

This species is a great flier, migrating from North Africa to Northern Europe.

20. SPOTTED LONGHORN
(RUTPELA MACULATA)

Many species of beetle visit flowers in search of nectar. All of them are day-flying insects and not particularly large. They move continually from one plant to another, because nectar is nutritious but available only in limited quantities.

LENGTH: 1½ in. (40 mm)
ORIGIN: Europe

The yellow and black of this beetle mimics the colors of a wasp. It's a good way of deceiving predators into thinking it is dangerous, although in fact it is quite harmless.

20

Bees have created one of the most complex and fascinating of all animal communities. This is why they are described as social insects. A single queen, living in the hive, lays eggs that will produce worker bees, which perform all the tasks required for the survival of the colony and drones (males), whose task is mating with new queens. When the colony grows to a certain size, new queens are produced and the old queen goes off with half the bees to start a new colony. The workers collect nectar and pollen from flowers. From the nectar they produce honey, on which the bees feed, and from honey and pollen they produce a substance that is used to feed the growing larvae. Honey has also been used by humans as a food and sweetener for thousands of years, which is why bees are kept all around the world and are of great economic importance.

21. HONEYBEE
(APIS MELLIFERA)

In the course of its life, every worker bee performs a well-defined series of functions. It begins with cleaning and maintenance tasks within the hive, and then, after a few weeks, it becomes a forager, going out to collect nectar and pollen from flowers. The bee consumes some of its food and brings the rest back to the hive, carrying the pollen in special "baskets" on its hind legs.

LENGTH: ½ in. (8 mm)

ORIGIN: Worldwide

⭐ **RECORD!** Most useful insect: Bees and other flower-loving insects help to pollinate at least one-third of the crops we eat.

21

To defend their colony, bees will inject venom, often leaving their barbed sting in the skin of the aggressor.

These hexagonal wax structures are known as combs. They are built by the worker bees to house the larvae and store honey.

THE DANCE OF THE BEES

How do worker bees tell each other the location of a food source like a woodland clearing with an abundance of flowers? Amazingly, they have their own special language, known as the "waggle dance," which includes both visual signals and smells. The scent of the flowers they have discovered is communicated to the other bees with their antennae. If the new source of food is nearby, say around 160 feet (50 m) from the hive, the bee performs a simple circular dance on the surface of the comb. If it is farther away, however, the bee performs a different dance, describing a sort of figure-eight pattern with pauses and much waggling of its abdomen. The other bees can work out the distance from the number of times the dancer turns in a given period of time and from the movements of its abdomen, which are more rapid if the source of nectar is nearby.

THE BEES' TREASURE: HONEY

The history of honey as a foodstuff goes back a very long way. We know that 5,000 years ago the ancient Egyptians practiced beekeeping, as did the Greeks and Romans, not only to get honey but also for wax (produced by the bees to build their combs), which was used to make writing tablets or as a base for soothing balms and ointments. Modern beekeeping has not changed all that much. It is still the bees that do most of the work, only now they are provided with an artificial house—the beehive.

The beekeeper knows how to handle his bees, but wears a protective bee suit to avoid getting stung.

Termite mounds rise like immense red-brown fortresses or castles. Termites are social insects (like ants and bees) that live in complex communities, rather like the kingdoms from ages ago. These kingdoms are founded on the division of labor. Individuals of the same species, but differing in size and appearance, perform their tasks for the good of the colony as a whole. Termite society includes soldiers with enormous jaws, constantly busy workers, and members that are able to fly, mate, and start new colonies. Termites may seem like ants, but the two groupings are unrelated. They belong to an order of their own, the Isoptera, which includes more than 2,500 species and is more closely related to the cockroaches.

THE TERMITARIUM

A single "castle" may be home to more than a million termites. The largest mounds, found across most of Southern Africa, are nearly 30 feet (9 m) in height and roughly 10 feet (3 m) across at the base. They also extend a couple of yards underground. The termites control the temperature and air circulation through a network of channels with openings on the sides of their tower—a perfect air-conditioning system.

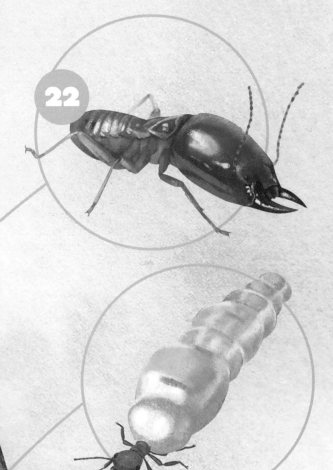

22. AFRICAN TERMITE
(MACROTERMES BELLICOSUS)

Soldier termites have a large head and powerful jaws to protect the nest and fight off ants, which are their sworn enemies. The soldiers' sole task is defense, while the workers are responsible for building and maintenance operations, gathering food, and acting as nurses to the larvae.

LENGTH: ½ in. (10 mm) (soldier termites)
ORIGIN: Africa

THE QUEEN

All the termites in a colony are offspring of a single queen, who spends her life laying eggs and may live for more than 30 years in a defended room within the mound. The much smaller king is always present and mates with her often.

THE INVENTION OF AGRICULTURE

Termites gather large amounts of wood and leaves, but do not eat this material, which is neither nutritious nor digestible. The wood is used to help grow a microscopic fungus that thrives only in termite mounds and is the insects' principal source of food.

When an animal dies, insects are the first creatures on the scene. Flies lay their eggs in the flesh of the dead animal, which hatch into maggots that consume the tissues of the corpse. Other insects soon arrive, especially beetles, whose entire life cycle takes place in the bodies of dead animals. There are also arthropods that eat the most disgusting things on earth. Dung beetles, for example, live off the excrement of herbivores (like cows), while millipedes consume fungi and rotting leaves.

The scarab's long, spiky front legs are useful for getting a good grip on the ground when it is rolling its ball of dung.

23

23. SACRED SCARAB
(SCARABAEUS SACER)

This beetle makes large balls from the dung of herbivores, rolls them to a hidden spot, then buries them. The females lay their eggs in the balls, where the larvae hatch and grow. Dung beetles, of which there are hundreds of species around the world, are therefore very useful in removing and recycling the excrement of herbivores.

LENGTH: 1¼ in. (30 mm)
ORIGIN: Africa

In the natural world, red stands for danger. It is often associated with poison. Millipedes get the toxic substances found in their bodies from the matter on which they feed.

24

24. FIRE MILLIPEDE
(APHISTOGONIULUS SP.)

Millipedes are not fussy eaters. They will eat dead plant matter, fungi, and both dry and green leaves. For this reason, they are very common and active in many tropical environments, especially at night. For protection, they rely on their armor and their coloring, which warns predators that their bodies contain toxic substances.

LENGTH: 6 in. (150 mm)
ORIGIN: Africa

25. BURYING BEETLE
(NICROPHORUS VESPILLO)

Attracted by smell, this beetle flies to the corpses of small vertebrates and begins digging under them, burying them in the soil. The females remain with the buried animal and lay their eggs in it. These beetles, together with other "undertaker" insects, are important in clearing away the corpses of animals that might otherwise spread disease.

LENGTH: ¾ in. (20 mm)
ORIGIN: North America

Some species of these beetles feed on other organic substances, including fungi and excrement.

25

A species akin to the previous one, *Nicrophorus humator*, has the same habits, but is completely black.

Beetles of the Silphidae family (carrion beetles) feed on the flesh of dead animals. Their flattened bodies enable them to push themselves underneath a corpse.

PREDATORS

Being a predator means surviving by eating other animals, which are often captured alive. The struggle for survival has resulted in an "arms race" between prey and predators, and this is particularly true among arthropods. If, for example, a beetle develops a thick shell, its natural enemies will tend to develop large, powerful jaws to overcome its defenses.

1. PRAYING MANTIS
(MANTIS RELIGIOSA)

The spiny hug of the mantis is a nightmare for small field insects. When its prey comes close, at a distance of 1 to 2 inches (3–5 cm), the mantis shoots out its arms and in less than a tenth of a second grasps its victim, like the butterfly in this illustration, of which only the wings remain uneaten. Mantises do not use poison but devour their victims alive, held fast in a fatal embrace.

LENGTH: 2¾ in. (70 mm)
ORIGIN: Europe

1

Mantises' large compound eyes give them a precise picture of what is going on nearby, in front of them and to either side.

2. SABER-TOOTHED GROUND BEETLE
(ANTHIA CINCTIPENNIS)

The head of this beetle is equipped with large pointed jaws, which it uses to smash the armor of smaller insects. A series of specialized organs, known as palps, enable it to manipulate the food in its mouth and hold it in place while chewing and sucking on it. The beetle's legs are for moving about quickly, not gripping its prey, as in the case of a mantis.

LENGTH: 2 in. (50 mm)
ORIGIN: Africa

The white markings on the black wing cases of this insect serve as a warning to predators of the presence of toxins.

2

3. JUNGLE CENTIPEDE
(SCOLOPENDRA SUBSPINIPES)

These large centipedes are some of the most impressive predators of tropical forests. Practically blind, they move about at night in search of insects and small vertebrates, which they track down to their hiding places using their sensitive antennae. To kill their prey, like the cockroach in the illustration, they pierce it with their sharp jaws and inject venom.

LENGTH: 10 in. (250 mm)
ORIGIN: Asia

3

The centipede's strong tapering legs are also useful for holding down its prey.

Ants, like other social insects, are generally small but often form very large groups. They manage to capture insects larger than themselves because they work together. Scientists have recently discovered that ants' nests are auto-organized systems, meaning that large colonies of individual insects are able to govern themselves without the need for a leader. In practice, every tiny ant obeys a few simple rules and responds to the stimuli of its companions. If a scout has found a source of food, it sends out a request for help in the form of special chemical signals, and ants nearby come running. If the helpers are still too few in number, other ants will send the same signal, calling up more ants. When the need has been met, the number of requests tails off and no further ants arrive, without anyone having to issue precise orders.

4

The swollen golden abdomens of these ants are full of sugary substances.

4. HONEYPOT ANT
(MYRMECOCYSTUS MEXICANUS)

In the deserts of North America, when food is hard to find, some worker ants of this species transform themselves into living food reserves for their companions. Needy worker ants request help with their antennae, and the "honeypot ants" pass food to them by giving a sort of kiss. These specialized workers are delicate and vulnerable, so they spend their whole lives in the ants' nest, hanging from the ceiling.

LENGTH: ¾ in. (15 mm)
ORIGIN: North America

5. DESERT ANT
(CATAGLYPHIS SP.)

Fast moving and heat resistant, *Cataglyphis* ants patrol on burning sand and rocks even in the middle of the day, capturing creatures that have been overcome by heatstroke. Scientists believe that they can find their way using the position of the sun.

LENGTH: ½ in. (8 mm)

ORIGIN: Africa

⭐ **RECORD!** Most heat-resistant animal: These ants survive on sand at temperatures up to 122°F (50°C).

Their long, slender legs allow these ants to run very fast on the burning sand.

The yellow and black banding of the wasp's body is another typical warning sign to predators.

6. WASP
(VESPULA VULGARIS)

Close cousins of the ants, but with the ability to fly, wasps prey on smaller insects. They chew wood to build combs and raise their larvae in the regular-shaped cells.

LENGTH: ½ in. (10 mm)

ORIGIN: Europe and Asia

nlike many other ants, army ants (*Eciton* genus) have no home but are part of a great army that marches on the ground through the forests of South America, constantly in search of prey.

⭐ **RECORD!** The greatest army: African driver ants (*Dorylus*) march in the largest numbers, often in a group of more than 1 million.

Army ants capture many insects, including other predators, such as spiders and scorpions, in bushes and shrubs.

The task of the workers, which come in two different sizes, is to capture prey and transport larvae and the queen.

The soldier ants, ¾ inch (15 mm) in length, have large jaws and a stinger, which they use to protect their companions.

F or some ants, vegetation may be a refuge or a source of food, but for others it is territory to be conquered. This is true of weaver ants of the *Oecophylla* genus, which live in the tropical forests of Africa and Asia. Unlike many other ants, they do not make their nest underground. They live on trees and use the leaves as building material for their nests.

7. WEAVER ANTS
(OECOPHYLLA SP.)
LENGTH: ½ in. (8 mm)
ORIGIN: Asia and Africa

BUILDING THE NEST

The nest is the real masterpiece of these ants, which fold leaves to construct it. Their larvae, transported by the workers, are able to secrete a sticky kind of silk, which they use as a natural glue: hence the name "weavers." Some of their nests house only workers and larvae, but those at the center of the colony may also accommodate a queen.

Every colony consists of more than a dozen of these nests, hidden by vegetation.

As soon as an intruder is identified, the ants arrive in large numbers to deal with it.

THE ATTACK

Their motto is "strength in numbers." These ants go after their victims in large groups, guided by the senses of sight and touch. To overcome their prey, they do not sting, but stop them with their strong jaws, damage their joints, and sprinkle them with formic acid, which attacks the insect's tissues.

THE QUEEN

After mating in flight, a new queen tears off her wings and hides under a leaf. She does not move or feed and must rely on the reserves she built up when still in her original ants' nest. Her goal is to lay her eggs and hatch out the first workers, who will then attend her, go out hunting, and build their first nest.

The first eggs of the queen that are hatched become the workers that will help to extend her empire.

Not all ants are predators. The leaf-cutter ants of South America (*Atta* genus) are a prime example. The most interesting aspect of their lives is that they do not eat the leaves they cut, but use them in another, truly unique, way.

The workers use their sharp jaws to cut off pieces of leaf, which they then carry back to the nest.

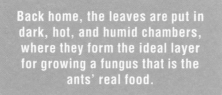
Back home, the leaves are put in dark, hot, and humid chambers, where they form the ideal layer for growing a fungus that is the ants' real food.

Wasps and hornets are the winged cousins of the ants. Like ants, they often live in colonies, but of smaller size. They have strong, sawlike jaws that they use to carve up insects and fruit. Armed with a sting at the end of their abdomen, which they use for defense or to kill prey, they can inflict a painful wound, even for a human being. This group includes some of the most dangerous insects in the world.

8

Bees are not stung to death but chopped up in the hornets' strong jaws.

Wasps work together to feed their larvae. Those that go out hunting bring back food for their companions in the nest.

8. ASIAN GIANT HORNET
(VESPA MANDARINIA)

Recognizable by their all-yellow heads, these enormous hornets are formidable bee hunters, taking their victims by surprise on flowers. Sometimes they will even go to the beehive to catch bees in larger numbers, since their armor protects them against the bees' stings. To defend themselves from these hornets, Japanese bees have perfected a system unique in the animal world. They surround the hornet in a tight-packed group and beat their wings in unison, raising the hornet's body temperature and killing it.

LENGTH: 1½ in. (40 mm)
ORIGIN: Asia

9. WARRIOR WASP
(SYNOECA SEPTENTRIONALIS)

These large black wasps make a nest shaped like a football or rugby ball out of wood that they have chewed. They raise their larvae in these nests. If the colony is threatened, each wasp can call the others by sending out chemical signals inviting them to attack the intruder. Their sting is one of the most painful of all wasp stings, on par with that of *Pepsis grossa* (see page 63).

LENGTH: 1¼ in. (30 mm)
ORIGIN: South America

Some of the insects with the most surprising life cycles are the solitary wasps, which do not live in colonies like most of their kind. In many cases, the females feed on nectar, but they also capture other arthropods as food for their larvae. Their methods would provide material for a horror movie.

The emerald cockroach wasp uses its sting as a precision weapon.

10

10. EMERALD COCKROACH WASP/ JEWEL WASP
(AMPULEX COMPRESSA)

When it finds a cockroach, this wasp stings it with a poison that freezes it for a few seconds. Then, accurately targeting the brain of her victim, she injects a second poison that inhibits the cockroach's instinct to escape. As a result, the wasp is able to take hold of the cockroach's antenna and lead it meekly back to its den, which is a burrow in the ground. Here the victim, unable to defend itself or attempt to escape, will serve as fresh food for the wasp's larva.

LENGTH: 1¼ in. (30 mm)

ORIGIN: Asia and Africa

11

11. GIANT ICHNEUMON
(RHYSSA PERSUASORIA)

The females of this large wasp species possess a very slender ovipositor that is longer than their bodies. They use it to pierce the bark of a tree and deposit an egg close to the larvae of other insects that live in rotting wood, such as the great capricorn beetle (page 34) or the giant wood wasp. The unfortunate insect becomes food for the ichneumon wasp's larva, which does not emerge from the tree until it has completed its metamorphosis.

LENGTH: 1½ in. (40 mm)

ORIGIN: Europe and Asia

12. TARANTULA HAWK WASP
(PEPSIS GROSSA)

One of the largest wasps in the world, *Pepsis* specializes in catching tarantulas, large tropical spiders, which it paralyzes with its poison. After poisoning a spider, it takes it back to its den and lays an egg in it. When the larva hatches out, it will feed on the paralyzed spider.

✪ **RECORD!** Most painful sting: The sting delivered by *Pepsis* is believed to be more painful than that of any other insect.

LENGTH: 1½ in. (40 mm)

ORIGIN: North America, South America

Although the wasp is smaller than the spider, it has the advantage of speed and often wins the battle between them.

Although not all spiders are web weavers, a spider's web is extraordinary. Thickness for thickness, it is stronger than steel. Circular or orb webs have been developed by spiders to catch flying insects. Their potential victims have responded by adopting some clever defenses. For instance, the "dust" on the wings of butterflies (in fact microscopic scales) is not to help them fly more efficiently, but to enable them to slip out of a spider's web more easily.

13

Deinopis is active only at night. In the daytime, it draws its legs in close to its body to disguise itself as a stem of grass.

13. NET-CASTING SPIDER/ GLADIATOR SPIDER
(DEINOPIS SP.)

The *Deinopis* species are unique among spiders in using their web as a "fishing net," cast by their front four legs. To cast its net in the darkness at just the right moment, the spider relies on its two large front-facing eyes, which are sensitive to the dim light of the moon and stars.

LENGTH: 1¼ in. (30 mm)

ORIGIN: Africa, Asia, and South America

At the center of their webs, some species create a silken design, known as a stabilatum. We still don't know why, but it may be useful in attracting certain insects.

14. SILVER ARGIOPE SPIDER
(ARGIOPE ARGENTATA)

A typical web 12 to 16 inches (30–40 cm) in diameter, as woven by the Argiope spider, requires some 100 feet (30 m) of silk filament a few thousandths of an inch in thickness. For an animal whose body measures a mere ¾ inch (20 mm), this is a large quantity of material. Spiders are therefore champions of recycling. When they need to spin a new web, they first eat their old one.

LENGTH: ¾ in. (20 mm)
ORIGIN: South America

Spiders of the Caerostris genus are masters of camouflage. When inactive, some species hold on to a twig and pretend to be a protruding piece of bark or a thorn.

15. DARWIN'S BARK SPIDER
(CAEROSTRIS DARWINI)

This spider weaves its web above water, where it can trap insects living in damp environments. The upper threads of the web, which is roughly 3 feet (1 m) in diameter, are stronger than the lower ones, the better to support the structure in strong winds.

LENGTH: ¾ in. (20 mm)
ORIGIN: Africa

✪ **RECORD!** The largest spider's web in the world is held by threads 50 to 65 feet (15–20 m) long, stretching from one bank of a river to the other.

The largest spiders create immense webs on which they spend most of their lives. In such cases, the web is not reconstructed every night, but simply repaired.

This 3 foot (1 m) wide web has a number of golden threads: They may serve to attract certain kinds of flying insects, which are then caught by the spider.

The large *Nephila* spiders of the tropics may have bodies 1½ inches (40 mm) in length. They are the largest spiders that use a web for hunting.

This is the male *Nephila*, which is much smaller than the female.

★ **RECORD** Strongest spider's web: The webs of the large *Nephila* species are strong enough to capture birds and bats.

Only some spider families use webs for hunting. Many others rely on launching lightning-fast attacks on their prey. Guided by sight or vibration, they rush forward, grab their victim, then bite it to inject poison. A good meal may last them several days, or even weeks. Most of these species are nocturnal, but some are also active in the daytime.

Some crab spiders are able to slowly change color when they move from flower to flower.

16. CRAB SPIDER
(THOMISUS ONUSTUS)

Crab spiders get their name from the sideways movements typical of this family of arachnids. Experts in laying an ambush, they conceal themselves on vegetation or flowers, ready to capture visiting insects. They then suddenly seize their prey in a deadly embrace, stopping the victim before it can get away.

LENGTH: ¾ in. (15 mm)
ORIGIN: Europe

16

17. ZEBRA BACK SPIDER
(SALTICUS SCENICUS)

With their eight eyes, two of which are large and forward-facing, the jumping spiders (Saltcidicae family) are an oddity even among spiders. Often colorful and small in size, they hunt their prey like miniature cats, ready to leap on their victims when they get within about ½ inch (8 mm). Unlike most other spiders, they are active in the daytime and rely completely on their sharp sight for hunting.

LENGTH: ½ in. (8 mm)
ORIGIN: Europe

Before making its final leap, the spider gets as close to the mosquito as possible, keeping it under close observation to figure out the distance between them.

17

18. GIANT CRAB SPIDER
(HETEROPODA BOIEI)

Keeping a low profile on tree trunks, these large spiders are common in tropical forests. When night falls, they lie in wait for insects and small vertebrates moving through the vegetation, springing on them when they are a few inches away. They detect their prey mainly through vibrations and movements of the air. Their sight plays only a secondary role.

LENGTH: 1½ in. (40 mm)

ORIGIN: Asia

18

During the day, these spiders hide under the bark and in the hollows of trees.

Known as the world's largest spiders, tarantulas (members of the Theraphosidae family) may be larger than a human hand. Typically found in tropical forests, they are active mainly at night, when they emerge from their hiding places to hunt insects, frogs, and geckos. Despite their size, they are not harmful to humans. Many smaller spiders have stronger poison.

> The fangs of this spider are almost ¾ inch (2 cm) in length, as long as those of many venomous snakes.

19

19. GOLIATH BIRDEATER (THERAPHOSA BLONDI)

These tarantulas may take four or five years to reach adulthood and may live to the age of 15. Unlike smaller spiders, tarantulas can go without food for months. But they are sensitive to water shortages, so during dry periods they withdraw into their burrows and seal the entrance with thick layers of silk. Though painful, the bite of this spider is not considered dangerous for humans.

LENGTH: 4¾ in. (120 mm)

ORIGIN: South America

✪ **RECORD!** The largest spider in the world: Tarantulas may weigh as much as 7 ounces (200 g) and have a leg span of around 12 inches (30 cm), the size of a dinner plate.

Urticating (itchy) hair
enlarged 200 times.

ITCHY HAIRS

The abdomens of South American tarantulas are covered in a large number of itchy (urticating) hairs. If they are enlarged 50 times, you can see that they have a series of microscopic spines. These are also irritating for humans, especially if they get into your eyes or nose. They provide a good defense against the small carnivorous mammals that live in the forest.

20

Some species of *Avicularia* are more vividly colored than other tarantulas. This may be because they are active in the daytime.

20. ANTILLES PINKTOE TARANTULA
(AVICULARIA VERSICOLOR)

Thanks to their strong legs and a body lighter than most tarantulas, these spiders are at home in the trees, where they build a shelter between leaves and bark, using thick layers of silk web. Because of their long body hair, some species of *Avicularia* can also walk on water and are therefore able to move from one tree to another in flooded areas.

LENGTH: 3¼ in. (80 mm)
ORIGIN: South America

There is an old saying that "Fortune favors the bold." Destiny, in other words, is on the side of those who dare to make courageous decisions. From what we can observe in the natural world, evolution seems to be in complete agreement with this saying. In the world of spiders, we find many species that have pushed themselves beyond the normal limits, developing ways of life different from those of most of their kind.

21

This is one of the largest European spiders, but it presents no danger to humans.

21. RAFT SPIDER (DOLOMEDES FIMBRIATUS)

Spiders are not generally fond of water, but this one is an exception. It lives on the edges of ponds and can dart under the surface of the water to catch small fish, aquatic insects, or tadpoles. It grabs them with its legs, then drags them onto waterborne vegetation and injects its poison. The raft spider cannot breathe underwater, however, so it is still very dependent on solid ground.

LENGTH: ¾ in. (20 mm)
ORIGIN: Europe

22

22. TRAPDOOR SPIDER
(LIPHISTIUS SP.)

Hidden in its burrow, the trapdoor spider sits and waits for its
prey, relying on silk threads on the outside to transmit vibrations
to its legs. The entrance to its burrow is completely sealed by
a trapdoor, making it impossible to detect, but the moment an
insect passes by, the spider rushes out, seizes it, and drags it
inside. The whole operation takes about 1 second!

LENGTH: 1½ in. (40 mm)

ORIGIN: Asia

The name "bolas" refers to a throwing weapon used for hunting in South America that has a number of balls connected by strong cord. This spider's hunting technique is similar.

23. BOLAS SPIDER
(MASTOPHORA HUTCHINSONI)

The bolas spider uses the silk it spins in a very creative way. It attaches a small ball of glue to a silk thread, which it swings with one of its legs. At night, it lies on a branch, giving off a scent that attracts the males of certain moths. When one of these approaches, the spider becomes aware of vibrations in the air and swings its ball of glue until it strikes and captures its prey.

LENGTH: ¾ in. (15 mm)
ORIGIN: South America

The diving bell spider is one of the very few species in which the male is larger than the female.

24. DIVING BELL SPIDER
(ARGYRONETA AQUATICA)

Although not closely related to the raft spider, this species has also made its home in well-oxygenated freshwater. It is the only spider that can live beneath the surface of a lake, breathing air that it brings down from the surface using a "diving bell" made of silk. It feeds on small aquatic insects, which it catches amid the submerged vegetation.

LENGTH: ¼ in. (15 mm)
ORIGIN: Europe

25. GIANT HAIRY SCORPION
(HADRURUS ARIZONENSIS)

Scorpions are nocturnal animals that hunt during the hours of darkness. Almost blind, they detect their prey by picking up vibrations transmitted through the ground, then seize their victims with their claws (technically known as pedipalps), before piercing them with their deadly sting.

LENGTH: 5½ in. (140 mm)

ORIGIN: North America

Scorpions are not sun lovers. At dawn they hide away in hollows and under rocks. Very few scorpion species are active in the daytime.

25

A number of insects and spiders use poison (or venom) to defend themselves or to attack their prey. Almost all spiders, for example, produce venom, but only in a very few cases are they harmful to human beings.

Other beetles similar to *Diamphidia* are almost as toxic, also due to the plants on which they feed.

26

26. BUSHMAN ARROW- POISON BEETLE
(DIAMPHIDIA SP.)

This harmless-looking beetle is one of the world's most toxic insects. Its body is loaded with deadly substances extracted from desert plants and concentrated in its tissues. The larvae are even more toxic than the adults. They are sought out by the San (Bushmen), the ancient hunting people of southern Africa, who dip their arrows in these insects to transform them into poison darts capable of killing the antelopes they rely on for food.

LENGTH: ¾ in. (20 mm)

ORIGIN: Africa

✪ **RECORD!** Most poisonous insect in the world: The poison of *Diamphidia* is particularly toxic for mammals. A single drop in the bloodstream can kill an adult human being.

27. BULLET ANT
(PARAPONERA CLAVATA)

These large ants live in colonies of several hundred in the great tropical forests, eating insects of all kinds. They usually hunt alone or in small groups, but can call up others if necessary. Their venomous bite is primarily a defensive weapon. If a human gets bitten, it is extremely painful but not fatal.

LENGTH: 1 in. (25 mm)

ORIGIN: South America

⭐ **RECORD!** Most painful insect bite: Together with the tarantula hawk wasp (*Pepsis grossa*, page 63), this ant is one of the insects whose bite is most feared.

Among some Amazonian peoples, adolescents undergo an initiation rite during which they allow themselves to be bitten by these ants in order to prove their strength.

27

The famous black widow got its name because the female of the species eats the male after mating.

28. SOUTHERN BLACK WIDOW
(LATRODECTUS MACTANS)

Known as one of the most venomous spiders, the black widow produces a toxin more powerful than that of a cobra. It is, however, a species of modest size and not aggressive, injecting its venom only in small quantities. It spends much of its time in its web, waiting for insects to become entangled. The red hourglass pattern on the abdomen of the female is a warning sign to predators. There are a number of similar species in various parts of the world.

LENGTH: ¾ in. (15 mm)
ORIGIN: North America

29. BRAZILIAN WANDERING SPIDER
(PHONEUTRIA NIGRIVENTER)

When frightened, this large tropical spider raises its front legs to display its orange and black warning colors. This warning is important because this is one of the most dangerous spiders in the world. Their bite is very painful, and in some instances, it can kill a person. It hunts insects and small vertebrates among the trees of tropical forests.

LENGTH: 1¾ in. (45 mm)
ORIGIN: South America

The hair on the spider's legs are very sensitive to air currents, which allow it to know when animals are on the move nearby.

29

Many predator insects have spiny arms, which are used to trap their prey.

30

Amblypygids have flattened bodies so that they can hide under tree bark and rocks.

30. TAILLESS WHIP SCORPION (DAMON DIADEMA)

These arachnids, of the Amblypigi order, are distant relatives of the true scorpions, capturing their prey with pedipalps (front body parts) very similar to the arms of a mantis. The limbs are flexible and equipped with long, tapering spines. They have a special pair of legs that they wave slowly in the darkness, like antennae, to pick up chemical signals and signs of movement, which allow them to find insects to eat.

LENGTH: 2 in. (50 mm)
ORIGIN: Africa

31. AFRICAN MANTIS
(SPHODROMANTIS LINEOLA)

The front legs of this mantis are equipped with spines to immobilize its prey. The mantis can shoot its legs forward and embrace its victim in less than one-tenth of a second, with an action similar to a switchblade. Once caught and lifted off the ground, the victim is quickly devoured by the mantis, which always spends a few moments cleaning its weapons after a meal.

LENGTH: 3¼ in. (80 mm)
ORIGIN: Africa

The mantis's eyes are very sensitive to movement, but if a potential victim freezes, the mantis will not be able to detect it.

32. WATER SCORPION/ WATER STICK INSECT
(RANATRA LINEARIS)

Some predatory aquatic insects of the Nepidae family, commonly called water scorpions, have developed organs similar to the front legs of a mantis for catching tadpoles and aquatic larvae. After seizing their prey, they suck out its body fluids using a beaklike structure, which first injects a poison to soften the victim's tissues.

LENGTH: 2¼ in. (60 mm)
ORIGIN: Europe

31

The rear end of the water scorpion is equipped with a snorkel that is used to draw air down from the surface.

32

Some arthropods have developed truly impressive mouthparts, with outsized jaws, to attack and dismantle (take apart) their prey. Some plant-eating insects and the famous stag beetle also have strong jaws, but they are only used in duels with rivals.

In emergencies, these ants can direct their jaws downward and snap them together against the ground, which catapults them long distances.

33

33. TRAP-JAW ANT
(ODONTOMACHUS HAEMATODUS)

These ants walk around with their jaws wide open. The moment they touch their prey, the jaws close at a speed of over 60 miles per hour (100 kph). This beats the reaction times of all other insects.

LENGTH: ½ in. (10 mm)

ORIGIN: South America

⭐ **RECORD!** Fastest bite: The jaw movement of *Odontomachus* is the fastest in the animal world.

These beetles are great travelers, but they are not able to fly. Their wing cases are fused together above the abdomen, which prevents the wings from being opened.

34. MANTICORA
(MANTICORA LATIPENNIS)

To cope with the armor of their prey, the tropical "tiger beetles" have developed the most powerful jaws of any insect, more impressive in the males. The male *Manticora* also uses these appendages to hold its partner tightly during mating, like a pair of pliers worked by well-developed muscles.

LENGTH: 2¼ in. (60 mm)

ORIGIN: Africa

34

Their first pair of limbs, the pedipalps, are covered in long, sensitive hairs, which are used to gather information as they approach their prey.

35

35. EGYPTIAN GIANT SOLPUGID/ CAMEL SPIDER
(GALEODES ARABS)

Like large hairy spiders, the species of the order Solifugae, of which the Egyptian giant solpugid is one, are desert-living arachnids, with two enormous chelicera (a feature of their mouthparts) similar to pliers. These nonvenomous structures can move independently and at great speed to cut up their prey, in particular insects and desert geckos. Despite their awesome appearance, these animals are not harmful to humans, although their bite can break the skin.

LENGTH: 2¼ in. (60 mm)

ORIGIN: Africa

⭐ **RECORD!** Most powerful bite: Proportional to their body weight, these invertebrates probably have the most powerful bite in the animal world.

36. JAPANESE TIGER BEETLE
(CICINDELA JAPONICA)

The jaws of these small hunting beetles are their main weapon. Species in the *Cicindela* genus rely on these jaws to attack the smaller field insects on which they feed. They run rapidly over the ground, taking off and flying short distances if necessary.

LENGTH: ¾ in. (20 mm)

ORIGIN: Asia

These small predators depend mainly on the sense of sight, relying on their large compound eyes.

36

Many insects have elongated, tubelike mouthparts (technically called a proboscis) that can be used for attacking prey or extracting blood from their victims. The food they eat, consisting of the victim's tissues, is sucked up through the same tube, but it has to be in liquid form. Mosquitoes and horseflies, some of the most disagreeable of insects, belong to this group.

37. HORNET ROBBERFLY
(ASILUS CRABRONIFORMIS)

These insects are related to flies, but at first sight they seem to have little in common with them. They are in fact voracious predators of other insects, diving down on them in flight and stabbing them with their stiff beaks. Their preferred victims are bees and other large flies.

LENGTH: 1¼ in. (30 mm)

ORIGIN: Europe

The markings of this species are similar to those of a hornet, which is a good way of protecting themselves from insect-eating birds.

Only the female mosquito "bites."
The male, harmless to humans,
has large feathery antennae.

38. COMMON HOUSE MOSQUITO
(CULEX PIPIENS)

These mosquitoes would undoubtedly win the prize for the world's most hated insect. Unfortunately for us, however, mosquitoes are also the most successful order of animals in warm and tropical countries. The secret of their success is their life cycle. Resilient and adaptable, they produce numerous offspring, which develop very quickly.

LENGTH: ¼ in. (6 mm)
ORIGIN: Worldwide

39. TWO-SPOTTED ASSASSIN BUG
(PLATYMERIS BIGUTTATUS)

These bugs prey on insects, especially grasshoppers and cockroaches. They attack suddenly and thrust their powerful, dart-shaped mouthparts into their victim, paralyzing it with their venomous saliva. Then, using the same equipment, they suck out its body fluids. They can spray their venom a distance of 8 inches (20 cm), but they are not hazardous to human beings.

LENGTH: 1½ in. (40 mm)
ORIGIN: Africa

The bright colors of assassin bugs, black with yellow and white markings, are a warning signal. It means they are poisonous.

There is something terrifying about a spider or insect that can attack a small mammal, a lizard, or a frog. We tend to think that such events are unnatural, but in tropical forests they happen all the time.

Large tropical spiders, such as the South American banana spider (*Cupiennius getazi*), have no hesitation in attacking small animals, like mice, or amphibians, like frogs. Much of their diet consists of insects, especially cockroaches and grasshoppers, but if the potential prey is the right size, they will go after it. These spiders, whose bodies are about 1½ inches (40 mm) in length, are guided by the movements of the young frogs or the vibrations imparted to the leaves by the croaking of the males.

The frogs are unaware of the presence of the spider if it stays still or moves only very slowly.

BEHAVIOR AND ADAPTATION

Many insects form alliances that cross species, providing important services to one another. These relationships are described as symbiotic. This means the relationships are helpful between two or three different organisms. However, the benefits are not always clear to the organisms involved, and some take an unfair advantage.

2

There is no benefit to the ants in this case. The cheating butterfly causes damage to their colony.

1

The larva of this hoverfly (Syrphidae, see adult on page 39) deceives ants by imitating their scent and devours the aphids in their care.

The strange limb on the head of these insects does not produce light, as scientists once thought. It is probably an ornament to attract members of its own species.

3

1. THE ANTS AND THE CATERPILLAR

The caterpillar of the large blue butterfly (*Maculinea arion*) engages in a surprising deception. Thanks to its size and smell, it can pass itself off as an ant larva and gets carried into the ants' nest, where it is protected and cared for. Once in the nest, it devours the larvae of its insect hosts before completing its metamorphosis and turning into a charming blue butterfly.

LENGTH: ½ in. (10 mm) (as a caterpillar)
ORIGIN: Europe

2. ANTS AND APHIDS

Ants are involved in some of the most sophisticated symbiotic relationships, forming close relations with plants and other insects. A large number of European species, including *Formica fusca*, farm or cultivate aphids, the insect pests we call greenflies or blackflies. In much the same way as humans farm sheep or cattle, the ants herd them as they "graze" (in this instance, sucking the sap of plants) and protect them from predators. In exchange, the aphids supply the ants with a sugary secretion from their abdomens that the ants enjoy.

LENGTH: ¼ in. (5 mm) (the largest aphids)
ORIGIN: Europe

3. THE COCKROACH AND THE PLANTHOPPER

Some cockroaches (*Dorylaea*) go around with these strange tropical insects called *Pyrops* (one of many genuses known as planthoppers), which suck the sap from plants using their syringelike beaks. They then excrete drops of a sugary substance from their abdomens, which is much appreciated by the cockroaches and sometimes also by geckos.

LENGTH: 2¼ in. (60 mm) (in the case of the planthopper)
ORIGIN: Asia

With many arthropods, there is a significant difference in size and weight between the male and the female. It all depends on the lifestyle of a particular species, but often the female is much bigger because she has to produce and house the eggs within her own body. In some cases, the difference is very striking, with the female 100 times heavier than the male.

The "rhinoceros" beetles are some of the strongest in the world. Their legs, which serve to grip the branch and push against another male, can lift several hundred times their own weight.

4

4. HERCULES BEETLE
(DYNASTES HERCULES)

When male beetles challenge one another to a duel to win a female, the male tends to be much bigger, because he has to fight off rivals. This favors the larger specimens, leading to a gradual evolutionary increase in size. The curious horns of these species come into play when a fight occurs. The two contenders square up to each other, trying to push their rival off the branch on which they are standing. The females, on the other hand, who choose the partner that shows the greatest prowess in these duels, have no need of such a weapon.

LENGTH: 6¼ in. (160 mm) (male); 2¼ in. (60 mm) (female)

ORIGIN: South America

5. MEDITERRANEAN BLACK WIDOW (LATRODECTUS TREDECIMGUTTATUS)

A big difference in size between the sexes is not typical of all spiders, but in some families, especially those in which the females spin a web to catch their prey, the difference is very evident. The male may well be small so as not to attract the attention of the female, who has to be large to produce so many eggs and, if the male is not careful, is likely to make a meal of him.

LENGTH: ¾ in. (20 mm) (female); ¼ in. (5 mm) (male)

ORIGIN: Europe

⭐ **RECORD!** Most dangerous love affair: The black widow often devours her companion once they have mated.

5

The female of the Mediterranean black widow has 13 large markings on her abdomen, which make her immediately recognizable. This is a clear danger signal, warning predators of the toxicity of her bite.

Female insects and spiders always try to choose the strongest and most resilient mates. For them, egg production is a long-term business, and they must be sure it is worth the effort. Attracting a mate, too, is a very serious matter, and these creatures will adopt every possible tactic to make a success of it.

6

Despite their fearsome appearance, stag beetles feed on plant sap and sugary substances.

6. STAG BEETLE
(LUCANUS CERVUS)

One of the largest and most spectacular of European insects, stag beetles owe their name to their large mandibles (jaws), which are similar to a deer's antlers and used for a similar purpose. Only the males possess them, and they are not for feeding but for grasping rivals, hoisting them into the air, and throwing them off the tree on which they are fighting. The largest males with the biggest mandibles clearly have an advantage in these fierce contests.

LENGTH: 3¼ in. (80 mm) (male);
2 in. (50 mm) (female)
ORIGIN: Europe

7. STALK-EYED FLY
(TELEOPSIS DALMANNI)

The eyes of the males of this species of fly, one of the strangest in the world, are separated by two long stalks. A single male oversees many females, which hang out on the roots of a tree, ready to get rid of any approaching rivals. These rivals can immediately figure out the size and strength of the resident male by observing the length and thickness of his eye stalks as he moves his head from side to side.

LENGTH: ½ in. (8 mm)

ORIGIN: Asia

7

The absurd eyes of these flies serve only for reproductive purposes, having no other part to play. The insects feed on fungi and small dead animals.

8

Observers have noted that, when resources are scarce, some spiders do not bother with a "mating gift," but wrap a little earth in some silk to deceive the female for a while.

8. NURSERY WEB SPIDER
(PISAURA MIRABILIS)

In the world of spiders, the aggressive nature of the female, almost always larger and stronger than the male, can lead to the early death of her companion. For this reason, the males of some arthropod species adopt a "mating gift" strategy. An excellent example is the nursery web spider, which, on approaching a female, offers her a small insect wrapped in silk to keep her occupied. The male often tries to recover the gift after mating so he can use it to attract another female!

LENGTH: ½ in. (10 mm) (male); ¾ in. (15 mm) (female)

ORIGIN: Europe

9. COASTAL PEACOCK SPIDER (MARATUS SPECIOSUS)

The males of this small jumping spider species use their spectacular markings to make a good impression on the females, which are larger and brown in color. They perform dances, waving their legs and abdomen in a surprisingly rhythmic way—a sight no less fascinating than the movements of certain tropical birds.

LENGTH: ¼ in. (5 mm)

ORIGIN: Australia

✪ **RECORD!** Most spectacular display: No other spider or insect performs so colorful and complex a dance as the *Maratus* spider.

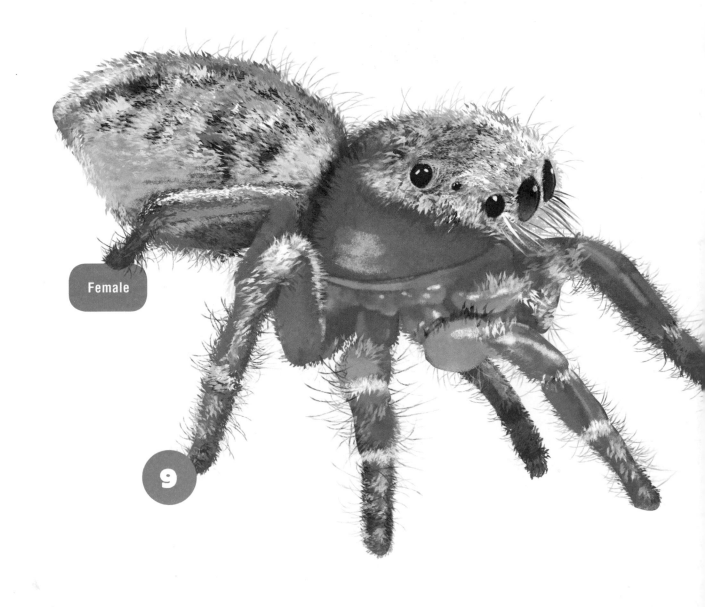

Female

9

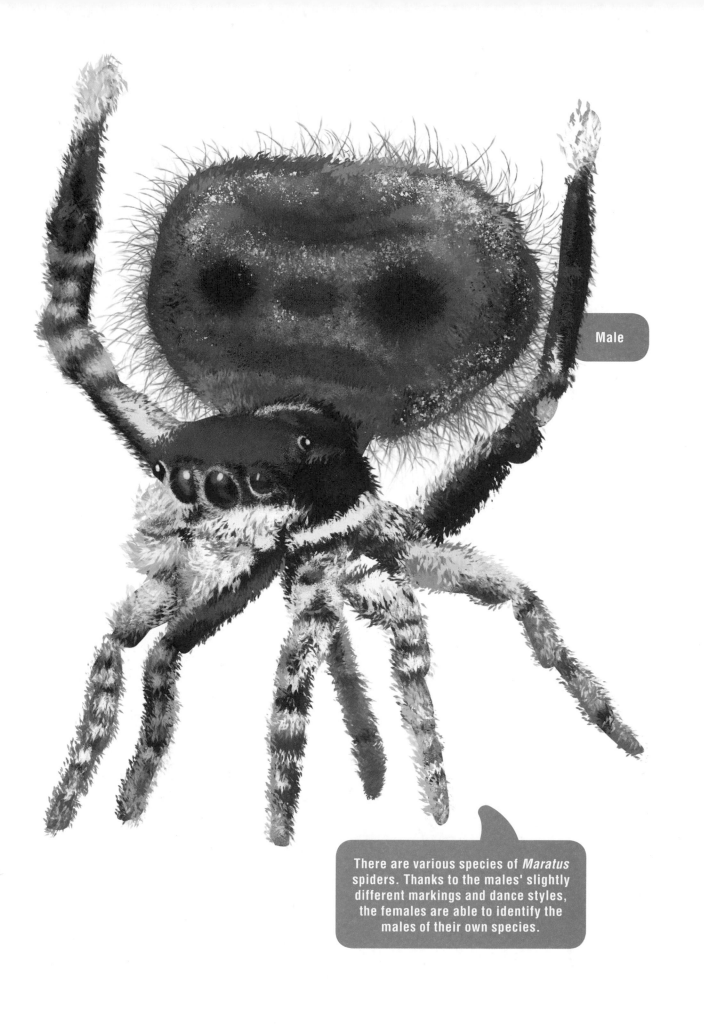

Male

There are various species of *Maratus* spiders. Thanks to the males' slightly different markings and dance styles, the females are able to identify the males of their own species.

Many insects are able to produce sounds, which sometimes can be quite loud. We think immediately of crickets and grasshoppers, but there are plenty of others. Singing is mainly a male activity, as the males show off their talents to the females of their species. In some cases, however, emitting a sound may be useful in scaring off a predator, especially when the noise comes as a surprise.

10

The large females of this species react immediately with a threatening display if they are surprised outside the burrow in which they usually hide.

10. KING BABOON SPIDER
(PELINOBIUS MUTICUS)

By rubbing together their two front pairs of limbs (pedipalps and chelicerae), which are ridged like a file, many large African tarantulas can produce an alarm sound to warn off intruders. As an additional defense measure, they rear up on their back legs, showing their long, poisonous fangs.

LENGTH: 3¼ in. (80 mm)
ORIGIN: Africa

11

11. BLADDER GRASSHOPPER
(BULLACRIS SP.)

These large grasshoppers produce sounds like many other insects in their order by rubbing their rear legs against ridged plates on their abdomens. This grasshopper's name refers to the fact that the male uses its large abdomen as an echo chamber to increase the sound of its musical output.

LENGTH: 2¼ in. (60 mm)
ORIGIN: Africa

The deep, swelling sounds produced by this insect can be heard 1¼ miles (2 km) away.

12. GIANT COLORFUL CICADA
(TACUA SPECIOSA)

Male cicadas are formidable "singers." The chirping of these insects is produced by strong muscles vibrating special plates in an air chamber. They do not rub one part of their body against another, like crickets, grasshoppers, and some spiders. Every species of cicada has its own recognizable call, which the females respond to in seeking a suitable mate.

LENGTH: 2 in. (50 mm)

ORIGIN: Asia

In some forests in Borneo, in Southeast Asia, there are cicadas that begin chirping for several minutes at exactly six o'clock in the evening. For people in the forest, they serve as a natural clock.

12

Many insects rely on smells, sounds, or colors when it comes to attracting females, but male fireflies are masters of light. Every species has its own particular pattern of light signals, which the females are able to recognize. The firefly's glow is a "cold" light, produced by highly efficient chemical reactions inside the insect's abdomen.

★ **RECORD!** The glow of the *Pyrophorus* genus of click beetles is the most intense light source produced by any insect.

Fireflies are most active at the beginning of summer, but only when it is really dark. The males emit an intermittent signal to attract the attention of potential mates.

The females respond to the males flying closest to them with a signal of their own.

The parents of young arthropods have often already died or are far away when their offspring hatch. Some species, however, devote a great deal of care to their young, protecting them during the first weeks of life.

13. GIANT FOREST SCORPION/ GIANT BLUE SCORPION (HETEROMETRUS SPINIFER)

Female scorpions are excellent mothers. As soon as the baby scorpions hatch, they move to their mother's abdomen and cling there for several weeks, protected by her mighty pincers and venomous sting. After their first molt, when they shed their skin, they climb down and become completely independent, now having to rely on their own resources for survival.

LENGTH: 6¼ in. (160 mm)

ORIGIN: Asia

13

Newborn scorpions are very light in color, which makes them easy to recognize.

Like scorpions, newly emerged centipedes also have a translucent body that does not darken until after the first molt.

14. JUNGLE CENTIPEDE
(SCOLOPENDRA SUBSPINIPES)

Centipedes, too, are good mothers, protecting and cleaning their eggs to prevent the growth of fungi. When the young hatch, the female coils herself around them and defends them against predators for the first week of life. In the larger species, it takes three years for the young centipedes to grow to adulthood.

LENGTH: 10 in. (250 mm)
ORIGIN: Asia

15. MONEY SPIDERS
(LINYPHIIDAE FAMILY)

The mother of these small spiders may already be dead when her tiny offspring emerge from their egg sac in the hundreds. To spread out as much as possible and thus minimize competition with their siblings, they spin a long thread of silk from their abdomens that acts like a kite. At the first breath of wind, it lifts the baby spider into the air and carries it away, often for 1 mile (1.6 km) or more, far from its birthplace. This enables the young spiders to colonize distant locations, including offshore islands.

LENGTH: ¼ in. (5 mm)
ORIGIN: Europe

Only the sedentary species that spin webs to hunt their prey become airborne this way.

Insects were the pioneers of flight. The first dragonflies, not very different from those we see today but the size of a hawk, were already flying 350 million years ago, long before the age of dinosaurs. Over the millions of years since then, wings have proved to be an extremely efficient means of movement and have been "adopted" by birds, mammals, and, to some extent, reptiles, amphibians, fish, and various invertebrates. Not all insects can fly, however. Many have lost the power of flight, and their wings have wasted away because they were not needed in the wider arthropod grouping, which includes spiders, scorpions, millipedes, centipedes, and crabs.

16

16. SMALL ELEPHANT HAWK MOTH
(DEILEPHILA PORCELLUS)

The nocturnal members of the hawk moth family (Sphingidae) are some of the greatest fliers of the insect world. Their four wings, powered by strong thoracic muscles, enable them to fly at more than 25 miles per hour (40 kph) and to hover motionless as they suck the nectar from flowers with their long proboscis. The hairy coat that covers their bodies keeps them warm when flying at night.

WINGSPAN: 2¼ in. (60 mm)

ORIGIN: Europe

There are many species of hawk moth, found in all parts of the world. This is one of the most colorful.

17

17. EUROPEAN ROSE CHAFER
(CETONIA AURATA)

Beetles, like this brightly colored specimen, are rarely great fliers. Their first pair of wings forms a protective shield, or wing case, while the second pair serves to keep them in the air. These wings, which are flexible and transparent, are normally kept folded away and are only used when the insect launches into flight. When the beetle lands, the wings are again folded away beneath their protective shield—a clever and practical strategy.

LENGTH: ¾ in. (20 mm)
ORIGIN: Europe

18

18. MADAGASCAN SUNSET MOTH
(CHRYSIRIDIA RHIPHEUS)

Regarded as one of the world's most beautiful butterflies (in fact a day-flying moth), this insect flies in the tropical forests of Madagascar, the great African island with many animal species that are not found anywhere else. Unlike many other butterflies and moths, its colors are mostly the result of light interference. This physical phenomenon is caused by the structure of the scales on its wings, which interact with visible light and change color depending on their angle.

WINGSPAN: 4 in. (100 mm)
ORIGIN: Africa

Butterflies retain their bright colors even after they have died. For this reason, they are much sought after by collectors.

utterflies, members of the Lepidoptera order, are one of the largest known groupings of insects, with more than 150,000 species distributed worldwide. All butterflies undergo an initial phase as caterpillars, eating large quantities of plant material (although a few are carnivorous), before sealing themselves in a chrysalis, from which the adult will eventually emerge. It is said that butterflies live only for a day, but this is rarely true. Most species survive for several weeks, and some for almost a year.

19. RAJAH BROOKE'S BIRDWING (TROGONOPTERA BROOKIANA)

This butterfly is so large that, from a distance, it could be mistaken for a bird. It can be found in the clearings of tropical forests, settling to suck nectar from the flowers of climbing plants. Its large, very long wings enable it to glide long distances, a habit not common among butterflies.

WINGSPAN: 8 in. (200 mm)

ORIGIN: Asia

19

The "dust" on butterflies' wings in fact consists of microscopic scales that overlap like the tiles on a roof. They give rise to the splendid patterns on butterflies' wings, and help them escape from spiders' webs: the drops of glue deposited on a web stick to the scales, which break away easily, allowing the butterfly to struggle free.

20. GIANT BLUE MORPHO
(MORPHO DIDIUS)

The wings of this butterfly show bright flashes of blue as it flies through the tropical forest. Like the wings of the Madagascan sunset moth (page 111), those of the morpho are iridescent, changing color depending on the angle from which they are viewed. Its colors are not due to pigments produced by the butterfly, but from the microscopic structures coating its wings.

WINGSPAN: 7 in. (180 mm)

ORIGIN: South America

⭐ **RECORD!** Butterflies with the most surprising colors: *Morpho* species, with their iridescent wings.

If the giant blue morpho settles and closes its wings, the bright blue disappears completely, leaving a brown coloration that blends in with the forest undergrowth.

Bats take the place of birds during the night, catching and killing large numbers of insects. These flying mammals use a sonar system (not radar) to capture their prey. As they beat their wings, they emit very high-frequency sounds (ultrasounds) and are guided by the echoes that bounce back to them off flying insects, even in complete darkness.

This American moth, *Bertholdia trigona*, has perfected an amazing defense. When a bat comes close, the insect emits a sound that disrupts the predator's hearing, preventing it from calculating the distance correctly. This often allows the moth to avoid capture in the nick of time.

★ **RECORD!** The most sophisticated system for avoiding capture in the insect world is the jamming system of the *Bertholdia* tussock moth.

In the case of bats, which hunt purely by sound, an insect's warning colors are no defense.

When the bat approaches its prey, the frequency increases, giving better "definition" and guiding it as it goes in for the kill. This is when the moth's jamming system is activated.

utterflies generally fly in the daytime, whereas moths fly by night and have markings that enable them to hide in vegetation when they are resting. There are many exceptions, though, and some moths have showy colors. The best way to distinguish butterflies from moths is to observe how they hold their wings when they are not flying. Butterflies hold them folded together above their bodies to mimic a leaf, whereas moths spread them over the surface they have settled upon.

21

The feathery antennae of the male Atlas moth picks up the chemical signals given off by females, especially in the dark.

21. ATLAS MOTH
(ATTACUS ATLAS)

The wings of the Atlas moth, one of the largest in the world, are decorated with an immediately recognizable series of elegant patterns. Despite its large size, this moth lives for only a few days, just long enough to mate. It has no mouthparts and is unable to feed.

WINGSPAN: 7 in. (180 mm)

ORIGIN: Asia

22

22. HAIRY TENTACLE MOTH
(CREATONOTOS GANGIS)

The amazing structures on the end of this moth's abdomen, resembling hairy tentacles, are scent organs, used by the males to spread chemical signals (pheromones) that will attract females. When the moth is at rest, the "tentacles" are limp and withdrawn into the abdomen, but they can be used when the time comes and the owner needs to give off his irresistible scent.

When its tentacles are being used, this moth is unable to fly.

WINGSPAN: 2 in. (50 mm)

ORIGIN: Asia

⭐ **RECORD!** Strangest moth: The weird tentacles on its abdomen make *Creatonotos* the oddest moth in the world.

23. DEATH'S-HEAD HAWK MOTH
(ACHERONTIA ATROPOS)

The death's-head hawk moth is a skilled burglar, breaking into beehives and stealing the bees' honey. It is able to deceive them, at least for a few minutes, by imitating their scent and thus getting around the guard bees that are supposed to be watching over the colony. This moth gets its name from the skull-like marking on its thorax.

WINGSPAN: 4¾ in. (120 mm)

ORIGIN: Europe and Asia

⭐ **RECORD!** Most sinister insect: No insect bears a more frightening symbol—a death's-head.

23

This insect can produce a loud whistle by compressing air in its proboscis, rather like a mouth organ.

Caterpillars, which are the larvae of butterflies and moths, spend all their time eating, until they are ready for their metamorphosis. Many plants have leaves with jagged edges to make it more difficult for caterpillars to feed on them. In fact, a caterpillar spends twice as much time consuming the edges of a jagged leaf as compared with a smooth one, because it is forced to continually change position. For many insectivorous (insect-eating) animals, there is no more desirable meal than a caterpillar. They are slow-moving, plump, and juicy. But caterpillars are not entirely passive and have developed some surprising ways of protecting themselves.

24

24. SPINY CATERPILLAR
(PSEUDAUTOMERIS SP.)

The stubby, compact shape of this caterpillar allows it to convert its body into a fortress of itchy spines to discourage other animals from attacking it. All these spines are inconvenient to carry around, but once on its food plant, the caterpillar does not need to travel around much.

LENGTH: 1½ in. (40 mm)
ORIGIN: South America

While some caterpillars rely on spines, others are equipped with long hairs that are very unpleasant if ingested or if they end up in a predator's nose and eyes.

25

25. PUSS MOTH
(CERURA VINULA)

This large fleshy caterpillar is the larva of the puss moth. In the daytime, it hides on light-colored tree bark, camouflaged against the branch or trunk. The two horns on the end of its abdomen are displayed only if the caterpillar is frightened. They release a strong acid to discourage insect-eating birds from attacking.

LENGTH: 2¼ in. (60 mm)
ORIGIN: Europe

Like all insects, caterpillars have six legs, although on the rear part of their bodies they also have additional "false legs," known as pseudopodia, which can grip onto twigs and branches.

There are tens of thousands of urticating hairs on these caterpillars' bodies, which cause itching and rashes.

26

26. PINE PROCESSIONARY
(THAUMETOPOEA PITYOCAMPA)

These caterpillars get their name because they move in procession. Each individual follows the next, so that the group remains together during migrations from one tree to another. Pine processionaries feed on pine needles and can be a serious problem, causing a lot of damage and undermining the health of the trees. The caterpillars gather in small groups during the winter in protective nests made of silk. The grayish adult moths emerge the following spring.

LENGTH: 2 in. (50 mm)
ORIGIN: Europe

Of all insects, dragonflies are the most feared aerial predators. They eat flies and mosquitoes, and sometimes butterflies and smaller dragonflies, which they catch on the wing. But they are also on the menu of various species of birds and spiders.

✪ **RECORD!** Fastest insect: Dragonflies like these are the world's fastest insects, able to fly more than 30 miles per hour (50 kph).

The larger dragonflies, such as *Anax imperator*, capture large quantities of flies, butterflies, and smaller dragonflies while they are in flight.

When it goes in for the kill, the dragonfly's legs form a kind of basket for catching its victim.

Bee-eating birds are fond of dragonflies and capture their wings with their tweezerlike beak.
Dragonflies live around lakes, rivers, and ponds because their larvae are aquatic predators.

Dragonflies are a symbol of the summertime. They fly rapidly over lakes and other bodies of water, but they are not as graceful as butterflies. The flight of a dragonfly is powerful and purposeful, and it may reach speeds of over 30 miles per hour (50 kph), which for an insect just an inch or so long is an absolute record. They can also hover motionless in the air and move in all directions, forward, sideways, and backward, rather like a helicopter. No animal of similar size, apart from a hummingbird or a hawk moth, comes anywhere near them in graceful flight.

27. SCARLET DRAGONFLY/ SCARLET DARTER
(CROCOTHEMIS ERYTHRAEA)

Flying like a red dart over the ponds and canals of much of Europe, this dragonfly is always a striking sight. This magnificent insect, with its bright red livery and powerful flight, feeds mainly on mosquitoes, flies, and other small flying insects, which it catches near lakes.

LENGTH: 2 in. (50 mm)

ORIGIN: Europe

27

This dragonfly is adapting well to climate change. In recent years it has extended its range in Europe, due to the milder winters.

28. BLUE-TAILED DAMSELFLY
(ISCHNURA ELEGANS)

When the time comes to mate, the male damselfly clasps the female, which is usually less brightly colored, at the back of the head with a pair of pincers located at the end of his abdomen. The female then brings her abdomen forward beneath her legs to join to the body of the male, forming the heart shape that these insects are known for.

LENGTH: 1½ in. (40 mm)

ORIGIN: Europe

Damselflies are able to fly while in this position, but not with their usual agility.

Damselflies also feed on flying insects but prey on smaller species.

29. FOREST GIANT DAMSELFLY
(MEGALOPREPUS CAERULATUS)

These insects are called damselflies because of their slender bodies and graceful flight. Dragonflies, which tend to be more powerfully built, hold their wings outstretched and parallel with the ground when they are at rest. Damselflies, on the other hand, keep their wings closed when not in use, rather like butterflies.

LENGTH: 6 in. (150 mm)

ORIGIN: South America

✪ **RECORD!** This is the largest dragonfly species in the world, though it owes most of its considerable length to its slender abdomen.

Dragonflies' wings appear fragile, but they are really quite strong. Many species beat their wings 20 times per second.

Beetles are not only one of the most successful types of insect but also one of the most numerous kinds of living organism, including plants. There are believed to be 350,000 beetle species, but no one can be really sure because new ones are being discovered all the time. One out of every four recorded creatures is a beetle! They all hatch from eggs to become larvae, and after a radical metamorphosis like that of the butterfly, they become hard-shelled insects with a seemingly infinite variety of shapes, sizes, and ways of life.

The larvae of these beetles, which burrow into timber, are also of impressive size: up to almost 8 inches (200 mm) in length.

30

30. GOLIATH BEETLE (GOLIATHUS ORIENTALIS)

Among the largest, most massive, and most spectacular of beetles, members of the *Goliathus* genus live in the forests of Africa. Slow and heavy on the wing, they rarely fly more than 65 to 100 feet (20–30 m). Goliath beetles feed on ripe fruits and the sap of trees. The males defend their territory by "headbutting" rivals, clearing the way for the arrival of possible mates.

LENGTH: 4¼ in. (110 mm)

ORIGIN: Africa

✪ **RECORD!** Heaviest beetle: Beetles of the *Goliathus* genus can weigh as much as 3½ ounces (100 grams), roughly a third of the weight of a can of soda.

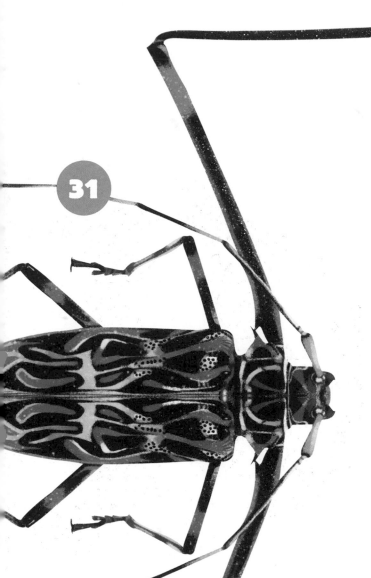

31. HARLEQUIN BEETLE
(ACROCINUS LONGIMANUS)

The male harlequin beetle from Amazonia is a giant whose legs, when fully outstretched, are usually longer than the beetle's entire body. As shown here, the males gather on the branches of trees in the tropical forest and compete for possession of the females, using their long legs to try to overthrow their rivals.

LENGTH: 4 in. (100 mm)
ORIGIN: South America

32. GIRAFFE WEEVIL
(TRACHELOPHORUS GIRAFFA)

The amazing shape of this beetle from Madagascar has earned it the common name of giraffe weevil. The male has the longest head of any insect and waves it about to charm potential partners. The female often chooses the largest male with the most elongated head and the most impressive movements.

LENGTH: 1¼ in. (30 mm)
ORIGIN: Africa

⭐ **RECORD!** Longest head: The giraffe weevil is the insect with the most elongated head.

Despite their large size, harlequin beetles are able to fly, although rather clumsily.

Females also have an elongated head, but it is only half as long as that of the males.

33

33. BLUE WEEVIL
(EUPHOLUS MAGNIFICUS)

As with some species of butterfly, the splendid colors of this beetle are mainly physical. This means the colors are created by the effect of light falling on the insect rather than colors of the insects themselves. Scientists still do not really understand the purpose of these brilliant markings but continue to study them.

LENGTH: 1¼ in. (30 mm)
ORIGIN: South America

The scientific term for the order of beetles, Coleoptera, derives from the Greek *coleos* (protective covering) and *pteron* (wing). It means "[creatures] with wings covered in armor." The front pairs of wings on a beetle have often been changed to become casings protecting their rear wings and abdomen. Not all beetles are able to fly, and some species rely on their heavy armor for defense or for survival in dry environments. Their armor plating reduces sweating, which helps them conserve precious body fluids.

34

The larva of this insect burrows into a tree and lives there for several years.

34. TITAN BEETLE
(TITANUS GIGANTEUS)

This rare beetle is more than 7 inches long and lives in the heart of the Amazonian rain forest. It has long antennae that are more developed in the male than in the female. It is harmless and feeds on tree sap, but it would be wise not to put your finger near its large, powerful jaws.

LENGTH: 7 in. (180 mm)

ORIGIN: South America

⊙ **RECORD!** Titanus giganteus is reckoned to be the largest insect in the world.

All carabid beetles rely on their strong jaws for capturing prey. Some are highly specialized and feed only on certain species, such as ladybugs.

35. CARABUS BEETLE
(CHRYSOCARABUS SPLENDENS)

The carabus beetle is one of the most predatory beetles. There are tens of thousands of Carabidae species (ground beetles) in all parts of the world, all with a similar body structure. Not all of them can fly, but they have spectacular markings, often in sparkling colors, which make them very attractive to collectors.

LENGTH: 1¼ in. (30 mm)

ORIGIN: Europe

36. SPINY LEAF BEETLE
(HISPA SP.)

This small beetle is protected from predators by spines made of chitin, the rigid substance that forms insects' body armor. It feeds on plant matter and is unable to fly. Its wing cases are bonded together for maximum protection.

LENGTH: ½ in. (8 mm)

ORIGIN: Europe and Asia

✪ **RECORD!** *Hispa* is the spiniest insect in the world.

Although heavily protected, these beetles are not immune to danger. Some species of spider entangle them in their webs and bite them where they are most vulnerable—the joints in their armor.

Making yourself invisible is the best way of avoiding predators. By using camouflage, some insects can blend themselves into their environment. For example, they may not only be the same color as a tree trunk but often can mimic the patterns of the material they are resting on or reduce the shadow they cast by flattening their body. The best camouflaged insects and spiders manage to copy the shapes of objects like stones, twigs, and both dry and green leaves.

37. BARK CRICKET
(ACANTHOSIS AQUILINA)

This tropical cricket not only has a sophisticated camouflage but they can keep completely still. These are both life-saving strategies. Insect hunters, such as birds, can create a mental image of their prey that enables them to see through the camouflage. The amazing markings of species that imitate every detail of tree bark make the process of recognizing the outline of an insect more difficult.

LENGTH: 2¼ in. (60 mm)

ORIGIN: South America

> The sharp spines on the hind legs of this cricket are its last line of defense should its camouflage fail.

37

38. RUNNING CRAB SPIDER
(PHILODROMIDAE FAMILY)

Being almost transparent, like this spider, is one of the best ways of escaping a predator. But this method works well only for small creatures with simple, slender bodies. And some parts of the body, such as the eyes or the digestive organs in the abdomen, can never be entirely see-through.

BODY LENGTH: ½ in. (10 mm)
ORIGIN: Africa

38

Tropical forests are home to various semitransparent insects and spiders, which often live on the underside of large leaves. The insects' camouflage is most effective when the sun is shining through the leaves.

Green leaves are the most obvious and abundant parts of a forest. For the small creatures that live in leafy environments, like forests, imitating these natural features has become a common practice. Large numbers of crickets, praying mantises, stick insects, and other bugs have learned to imitate green leaves, and many more are skilled at mimicking dry foliage.

Many of these creatures can also imitate the thorns of plants, giving them even more camouflage and protection.

39. LEAF-MIMIC KATYDID/ BUSH CRICKET
(TYPOPHYLLUM SP.)

Leaf-mimicking crickets live in the thick vegetation of tropical forests, even in the tops of trees, where they hide away as best they can. They use their wings to glide short distances but are not active fliers like other cricket species. They prefer walking to jumping, because their leafy disguise reduces their agility.

LENGTH: 3¼ in. (80 mm)
ORIGIN: South America

These insects use their long antennae for sniffing the surrounding vegetation without having to move and thus give themselves away.

39

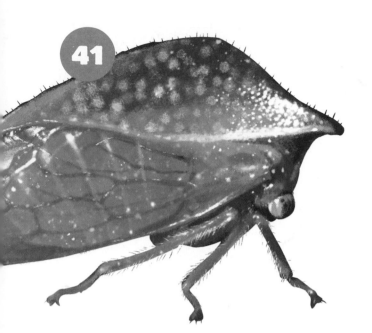

40. LEAF-MIMIC KATYDID
(MIMETICA SP.)

Some tropical crickets have sacrificed their ability to jump and fly in order to imitate leaves. Their wings have been modified to resemble plant matter in every detail, so that even close up it is difficult to tell them apart from real leaves. Their legs, too, have a flattened appearance, so that they merge into the background or blend in with the insect's body.

LENGTH: 2 in. (50 mm)
ORIGIN: South America

41. BUFFALO TREEHOPPER
(STICTOCEPHALA TAURINA)

Treehoppers are also great imitators of forest foliage. Since they are small in size, these insects pretend to be buds or small damaged leaves. They spend their lives on a food plant, and feed on the sap they extract from leaves using their strong pointed beaks.

LENGTH: ½ in. (10 mm)
ORIGIN: North America

Though leaf-mimic katydids hide among dead and dying vegetation, they feed on living plants, mainly at night.

40

42

42. LEAF INSECT
(PHYLLIUM COELEBICUM)

Every detail of a leaf is reproduced in the body of this special kind of stick insect. They not only have the shape and color of leaves, but also the veining and the imperfections at the edges. These insects live among the foliage of tropical forests and are most active at night, thus avoiding many predators.

LENGTH: 4 in. (100 mm)

ORIGIN: Asia

✪ **RECORD!** Best imitation of a plant: No insect can compare with the Phyllium species in mimicking the appearance of a leaf.

The eggs of these leaf insects look exactly like the seeds of poisonous plants, so they are avoided by other animals.

Trees and branches provide excellent cover, but to be really invisible you need to transform your body in various ways. Many of the insects that conceal themselves in these environments have long, slender bodies and a delicate structure that make them very vulnerable. They rely on keeping absolutely still to avoid discovery.

43

When it moves, this mantis tends to sway slightly, like a twig in the wind.

43. GIANT AFRICAN STICK MANTIS
(HETEROCHAETA ORIENTALIS)

A number of mantis species try to imitate twigs, but none succeeds better than this insect, with its thin body and irregular abdomen that mimics the pattern of bark. To further confuse predators, it sometimes holds its legs outstretched in a cross position to change its outline. Even its eyes are pointed to resemble thorns, while its antennae are short and very thin.

LENGTH: 6 in. (150 mm)
ORIGIN: Africa

The appearance of this spider when active, casting its web, is completely different (see page 64).

44

44. NET-CASTING SPIDER/ GLADIATOR SPIDER (DEINOPIS SP.)

When not hunting, in the daytime, *Deinopis* spiders eat their own webs (to recycle the raw material) and stretch themselves out, holding their legs close together, until they look like a dry twig. This makes them almost invisible among the chaotic vegetation of the forests where they live. To strengthen the illusion, they will not budge, even if they are touched.

LENGTH: 1¼ in. (30 mm)

ORIGIN: Africa, Asia, South America

45

45. GIANT STICK INSECT (PHASMA GIGAS)

Twiglike in appearance, this insect can remain completely invisible, despite its enormous size. To maintain the illusion, it remains motionless for most of the day, feeding on leaves during the night, when the risk of attracting attention is greatly reduced.

LENGTH: 13¾ in. (350 mm)

ORIGIN: Asia

⭐ **RECORD!** Longest insect: 13¾ inches (350 mm) in length, this stick insect is probably the longest in the world.

This insect suddenly opens its colorful wings to frighten predators. But this is pure bluff, as the stick insect has no other means of defense.

As we have seen, many creatures specialize in imitating leaves, twigs, or pieces of bark. Some, however, mimic natural phenomena that are attractive to other insects, their aim being to draw them in and devour them. This is a kind of behavior known as offensive (as opposed to defensive) camouflage.

46

Newborn orchid mantises mimic small orange and black toxic bugs as a way of discouraging predators.

46. ORCHID MANTIS/ WALKING FLOWER MANTIS (HYMENOPUS CORONATUS)

One of the most spectacular disguises is that of the orchid mantis, every section of whose body mimics some detail of the orchid flower. Its legs possess swellings similar to petals, while its head resembles the reproductive organs of the orchid. These mantises do not always hide away among the flowers, but often station themselves in full view on a plant, so as to attract curious flies and butterflies, which are caught when they approach.

LENGTH: 2¼ in. (60 mm)

ORIGIN: Asia

⭐ **RECORD!** Best imitation of a flower: The orchid mantis reproduces every detail of the attractive parts of a flower.

47

It has recently been discovered that *Phrynarachne* also release chemical substances similar to those of real bird feces, the better to attract its prey.

47. BIRD-DROPPING SPIDER
(PHRYNARACHNE DECIPIENS)

Sometimes the art of camouflage takes a really unusual turn, as in the case of creatures that have evolved to resemble bird droppings. The champion of this kind of deception is this compact, smooth-bodied spider with irregular white and brown markings. It uses its web and the remains of its prey to create a splash similar to a dropping on the leaf where it lies in wait.

LENGTH: ¾ in. (15 mm)
ORIGIN: Asia

Many insects and spiders rely on markings of various colors to warn their enemies of the risks they run in attacking them. Some, like these species from Amazonia, can deploy strong poisons or have toxic flesh.

Members of the genus of tiger moths known as *Arctia* extract toxins from the plants they feed on at the caterpillar stage. The adults, too, are toxic and advertise the fact with their bright colors.

The curious zigzag pattern on these *Erotylus incomparabilis* beetles warns of toxins, produced because they eat certain forest fungi.

Spiny *Micrathena* spiders lie in wait in full view on their webs. Their yellow and black or red and black coloration announces that they can inflict a poisonous bite and have stiff, sharp spines. Better not mess with them!

Some harmless animals, especially insects, try to resemble dangerous species as closely as possible in order to deceive predators. In some cases, the imitation is almost perfect. In others, the resemblance is only approximate, but it may be enough to make the attacker hesitate, allowing the victim to escape. To be really safe, the insect must imitate dangerous creatures that are present in large numbers and are easily recognizable.

As well as having a painful sting, hornets possess strong jaws.

48

48. EUROPEAN HORNET
(VESPA CRABRO)

A near relative of the wasps, the hornet is one of Europe's most feared insects, because it can inflict a very painful sting. Hornets are social insects and are very widespread, sometimes living close to human settlements. This makes them a good model for various species of insects, which imitate them to ensure their own protection.

LENGTH: 1¼ in. (30 mm)
ORIGIN: Europe

49

To get maximum benefit from its imitation, this moth flies in the daytime, just like a hornet.

49. HORNET MOTH/ HORNET CLEARWING (SESIA APIFORMIS)

This unusual moth mimics the hornet in size, in the way it flies, and in the sound it makes. Because of that, the insect, which feeds on nectar from flowers and is completely harmless, enjoys protection from predators, which mistake it for its dangerous counterpart.

LENGTH: 1¼ in. (30 mm)
ORIGIN: Europe

Many of these poisonous butterflies fly rather slowly to ensure their poisonous markings are easily recognized by the birds that might otherwise make a meal of them.

50

50. HARMONIA TIGER
(TITHOREA HARMONIA)

There are more than 100 species of butterfly that use a wing pattern of black stripes on a yellow and orange background as camouflage. Some of these species, including those of the *Tithorea* genus, are protected by chemical substances they get from plants during the caterpillar stage.

WINGSPAN: 2¼ in. (60 mm)
ORIGIN: South America

Butterfly species that rely on imitation are not closely related to the species they imitate.

51. EUNICE CRESCENT/ TIGER CRESCENT
(ERESIA EUNICE)

Certain species of nonpoisonous butterflies mimic the markings of their protected counterparts (those with toxic body fluids). Very often, models and imitators live in the same environments and have the same habits, making life difficult for insect-eating birds. Those birds that have had an experience eating a toxic butterfly avoid all butterflies with similar markings.

WINGSPAN: 2¼ in. (60 mm)
ORIGIN: South America

When insects that are poisonous or have toxic body fluids tend to have similar color schemes and showy markings, predators learn to recognize these combinations and to avoid them. These combinations tend to feature strongly contrasting colors: red and black, yellow and black, or white and black. Many protected insects and spiders tend to have similar color schemes.

52

> There are many different species of wasp, but most share the same distinctive yellow and black colors.

52. WASP
(VESPULA VULGARIS)

Wasps, with their conspicuous yellow and black markings, are easily recognizable. Their color scheme is immediately associated with their sting, which they are quick to use. For this reason, they are one of the most frequently imitated insects.

LENGTH: ½ in. (10 mm)
ORIGIN: Europe

> These spiders hunt using a circular (orb) web and are therefore very exposed to attack.

53. WASP SPIDER
(ARGIOPE BRUENNICHI)

Known as the wasp spider because of its distinctive color scheme, *Argiope* is one of the largest and flashiest European spiders. Its poison is not particularly strong, nor is it aggressive, but the yellow and black color scheme keeps attackers away.

LENGTH: ¾ in. (20 mm)
ORIGIN: Europe

53

54. REDBACK SPIDER/ AUSTRALIAN BLACK WIDOW
(LATRODECTUS HASSELTI)

The black widow spiders (*Latrodectus* genus) are some of the most venomous insects. There are various species in different parts of the world, but most are characterized by easily recognizable red markings on a black background. They weave their webs at ground level, even in very dry locations, and feed on insects, especially beetles.

LENGTH: ¾ in. (20 mm)

ORIGIN: Oceania

All the other black widows featured in this book have similar red and black markings.

55. STRIPED BUG/MINSTREL BUG
(GRAPHOSOMA ITALICUM)

These easily recognizable beetles have poisonous body fluids and are avoided by most other animals. They rely on their red-and-black-striped "jersey," which is also characteristic of many other poisonous insects and spiders, to keep attackers away. They feed on the sap of plants, including those less attractive to other plant eaters.

LENGTH: ½ in. (12 mm)

ORIGIN: Europe

Many tropical beetles of this kind combine orange with their yellow and black markings.

f strategies for making themselves invisible or escaping with speed fail, many insects have a second line of defense: putting on a threatening display. In many cases, this means flashing brightly colored false eyes that mimic the eyes of larger predators, such as hawks, owls, or carnivorous mammals.

The snake-mimic caterpillar (*Hemeroplanes triptolemus*) pretends to be a viper, displaying the false eyes on either side of its body and assuming a threatening pose.

The giant owl butterfly (*Caligo idomeneus*) relies on the false eyes on its wings, which even have highlighted "pupils," to trick predators.

If the peacock katydid (*Pterochroza ocellata*) is disturbed, it suddenly opens its wings to display its striking false eyes.

149

Ants are the world's most abundant insects. Many have a poisonous bite and an unpleasant taste. For this reason, they are not on the menu of all insect eaters, but only of "ant specialists"—some species of reptile, anteaters, and woodpeckers. Looking like an ant is therefore a good way to avoid getting eaten. Many small insects and spiders, especially in the tropics, where ants are very common, mimic ants.

This is a *Pseudomyrmex* ant, the model.

This is an ant-mimicking jumping spider (*Synemosina*), the imitator.

SPIDER OR ANT?

Some jumping spiders can mimic ants in every detail. They have even learned to hold their first pair of legs outstretched to simulate ant antennae. The *Myrmarachne* genus, for example, includes more than 100 species, all excellent ant impersonators, which sometimes gather in groups of 10 or more to look like ant colonies.

BUG OR ANT?

Several other kinds of insect also imitate
ants. Some of the most impressive are small
bugs, like this *Alydus*, but the imitators also
include the young of some tropical mantises
and a number of flies. In the case of flies, the
imitations are not as accurate, but they do
allow some degree of protection.

To be effective, a defense system doesn't need to be deadly. Sometimes it is enough to scare the predator, giving the potential victim time to escape. Among the insects and spiders, we find some of the weirdest and most wonderful systems for warding off predators.

56

The sticky substance sprayed by these termites does not travel much more than 1 inch (25 mm), but this is enough to stop other small insects.

The foam is effective because it has a nasty taste that spoils the flavor and aroma of the predator's intended meal.

56. NOZZLE-HEADED TERMITE
(NASUTITERMES SP.)

Termites are social insects that have a group of soldier termites, which are responsible for defending their nest. Soldier termites often have armored heads and strong jaws, but this species has a far more original defense system. Their elongated heads house a "cannon" that sprays a sticky, irritating substance at aggressors. They use this weapon mainly against ants, their great enemies.

LENGTH: ¼ in. (5 mm)

ORIGIN: Asia, Africa, and South America

57. SPOTTED GRASSHOPPER
(AULARCHES MILIARIS)

57

This grasshopper has glands in its thorax containing toxic substances. In less than 10 seconds they can produce a clearly visible yellow toxic foam that repels many predators, including birds and spiders.

LENGTH: 2¼ in. (60 mm)

ORIGIN: Asia

58. BOMBARDIER BEETLE
(BRACHINUS CREPITANS)

This beetle has one of the most effective of all defense systems. It is not able to fly, but its wing cases (the rigid shields protecting the abdomen) cover up glands that produce two different chemical substances. When the beetle is disturbed, it releases both of these compounds into a single chamber at the end of its abdomen. This causes an explosive chemical reaction, ejecting a substance that burns and injures predators.

LENGTH: ¾ in. (15 mm)

ORIGIN: Europe

✪ **RECORD!** The bombardier beetle has the most ingenious insect defense system: blowing up an attacker.

The chemical reaction produced by this beetle causes an audible explosion and a 212°F (100°C) cloud of gas, fatal for small predators such as ants.

The curious "door" on the spider's abdomen is made of chitin, the rigid substance that forms its exoskeleton (external covering).

59. CORK-LID TRAPDOOR SPIDER
(CYCLOCOSMIA SP.)

Many spiders excavate tunnels and close them with a plug of earth or silk (see page 75). This species has a more unusual technique. The final section of its abdomen forms a kind of armored door, which it can use to close the entrance to its burrow in an emergency. This clever solution prevents predators, like centipedes, which can normally break in almost anywhere.

LENGTH: 1¼ in. (30 mm)

ORIGIN: North America

nsects are found everywhere, but unfortunately their numbers have collapsed in recent years, especially in more developed countries. This is due to the destruction of their habitat to make room for intensive agriculture and urban development, as well as the widespread use of modern pesticides.

Even so, they are still plentiful. For every human being on Earth, there are said to be roughly 330 pounds (150 kg) of insects.

Helicopters are often used to spray insecticides (chemicals that kill insects), but this practice also destroys many species that are useful to humans.

Butterflies, like this painted lady, assist in the reproduction of plants and flowers.

The praying mantis is an efficient predator that feeds on harmful insects, including flies and mosquitoes.

Predators that specialize in catching aphids, like this lacewing, are some of the gardener's best friends.

155

Insects have adapted to eat almost anything, including the food crops grown by farmers, and some can transmit serious illnesses. From farmers' point of view, then, some must be viewed as pests. But the farmers' best allies in the fight against these species are often other insects that prey on them.

1. HONEYBEE
(APIS MELLIFERA)

Not only do these insects produce honey, which humans have been consuming for centuries thanks to the efforts of beekeepers, but they also help in the pollination of many plants, including those we grow for food. In moving from one flower to another in search of nectar and pollen, they also perform an essential service for farmers. In places where bees have almost disappeared, this work has to be done manually by teams of workers equipped with tiny paintbrushes.

LENGTH: ½ in. (8 mm)
ORIGIN: Worldwide

Useful insect

Unfortunately, bee numbers have fallen drastically in the last 20 years. This is due largely to monoculture (growing only one crop in an area), which prevents the insects from finding enough food. The use of insecticides, which weaken the bees and make them vulnerable to disease and parasites, also has contributed to their falling numbers.

Insect pest

There is no vaccine against malaria, only drugs that are partially successful in preventing the disease.

2. MARSH MOSQUITO
(ANOPHELES SP.)

This mosquito, more common in tropical countries, may be carrying a microorganism, *Plasmodium*, in its saliva glands. When the mosquito bites someone, this parasite enters their bloodstream, causing a high temperature and other unpleasant symptoms of malaria. Malaria can be cured, but it is still a dangerous disease, especially in some parts of Africa.

LENGTH: ½ in. (8 mm)

ORIGIN: Worldwide

⭐ **RECORD!** Most dangerous insect: Approximately 400,000 people die each year from malaria, mostly in Africa.

Insecticides are used to eliminate the Colorado potato beetle, but these are also harmful to many other animals. Unfortunately, the beetle's natural predators are not enough to deal with serious infestations.

3

Insect pest

3. COLORADO POTATO BEETLE
(LEPTINOTARSA DECEMLINEATA)

This beetle, originally from Mexico, first arrived in Europe in the middle of the last century and has spread throughout the temperate zone. It is particularly damaging because the larvae attack potato crops, which are an important food source for humans. In one year, a single pair of beetles can produce millions of offspring if nothing is done to stop them.

LENGTH: ½ in. (12 mm)

ORIGIN: North America, Europe, Asia

Useful insect

Ladybugs are so useful that some firms sell them to wage "biological war" on aphids.

4. SEVEN-SPOT LADYBUG
(COCCINELLA SEPTEMPUNCTATA)

As both larvae and adults, the brightly colored ladybugs are strong predators of aphids (greenfly and blackfly). They can consume dozens of aphids in a single day, so long as aphid-protecting ants do not intervene to prevent them (see page 95).

LENGTH: ½ in. (8 mm)

ORIGIN: Europe

When an organism is taken from its place of origin and introduced into a new environment, it may increase and spread without any control. Because they are so small, insects are often moved from one continent to another without anyone knowing. In some cases, newly introduced species can become invasive, causing problems for humans and other creatures. All the insects on this page are on the list of the world's 100 most dangerous invasive species.

5

Efforts to control the citrus beetle rely on wasps, which sometimes attack its larvae.

5. CITRUS LONG-HORNED BEETLE (ANOPLOPHORA CHINENSIS)

Imported into Europe and North America with shipments of timber from Asia, this large and showy beetle lays its eggs in large trees, such as beech and maple, particularly in gardens and city parks. The larvae burrow into the wood, weakening the infested trees, which then have to be cut down. Even if the damage is not terrible in the short term, it makes the trees vulnerable to disease and the inroads of less aggressive species.

LENGTH: 1½ in. (40 mm)

ORIGIN: Asia, introduced into Europe and North America

6. RED IMPORTED FIRE ANT
(SOLENOPSIS INVICTA)

Despite their innocent appearance, these red ants are a real pest in parts of North America, where they were introduced by mistake. They form enormous colonies, especially in cities, gardens, and the countryside, driving out other species of ant. As their name suggests, red fire ants can inflict a painful burning bite, enough to ruin many a picnic and outdoor activity.

LENGTH: ¼ in. (5 mm)

ORIGIN: South America, introduced into North America

7

Traps containing special chemicals are often used to deal with these insects. The beetles are attracted to the traps and killed before they can lay their eggs.

7. RED PALM WEEVIL (RHYNCHOPHORUS FERRUGINEUS)

This beetle from Asia threatens the tall palm trees of many cities in Southern Europe. The larvae burrow into the tree for four to eight months, causing the leaf fronds to suddenly fall. At this point, nothing can be done to save the tree. It is therefore difficult to identify threatened trees unless the infestation is very serious.

LENGTH: ¾ in. (20 mm)

ORIGIN: Asia, introduced into Europe

8. ASIAN TIGER MOSQUITO
(AEDES ALBOPICTUS)

During the 1990s, tiger mosquitoes colonized many countries, traveling in shipments of tires imported from Asia. The tires (if uncovered) almost always contain enough water for the larvae to develop in. Unlike many other mosquitoes, tigers are also active in the daytime, especially in the late afternoon, and can complete their life cycle even in fairly dry places, because the larvae develop so quickly.

LENGTH: ½ in. (8 mm)

ORIGIN: Asia, introduced worldwide

8

The most effective measures to combat tiger mosquitoes involve the use of bacteria that attack their larvae, a means of biological control.

Because there are so many insect species, and because they are so diverse, studying them is a complicated business. Entomologists, the scientists who undertake this work, require specialized training and knowledge. Often, they specialize in particular groups of insects (butterflies, mantises, or a single family of beetles), studying their behavior and relationships with other plants and animals, as well as describing newly discovered species. Every year, thousands of new species of insects, previously unknown to science, are recorded.

In the Labratory

MICROSCOPE

Some insects are very small. To observe them in detail, you will need a binocular microscope (one with two eyepieces), which allows you to observe your specimens without your eyes getting tired. It magnifies to the power of 50, giving you an image of excellent quality.

COMPUTER

Nowadays, all information from insect research is recorded on computers. When connected to special equipment for reading genetic code, computers can also compare different species and tell you how closely they are related.

PINS AND OTHER ITEMS FOR SETTING INSECTS

To display dead insects, collectors use special pins that set them in the best position, with legs apart and wings open. If they are kept in the right conditions, insects can be preserved for decades.

INSECT COLLECTION

Insects are sometimes captured, conserved, and placed in an entomological collection in a museum. This enables specialists from all over the world to visit the collection, study the insects, and spot even the smallest differences between the various species.

HEADLAMP

Many insects are nocturnal, so a lamp you can wear on your head to light the ground and surrounding vegetation is very useful so you can leave your hands free.

GUIDEBOOK

A guidebook for identifying the different species is essential, even when you are out in the field. It is difficult to memorize everything, and it is not uncommon to come across something you have never seen before.

ASPIRATOR

This device is for sucking up small insects, as you would do with a straw. The glass chamber between the two flexible tubes enables you to observe the insects you have captured and ensures that they do not go straight into your mouth!

NET

Essential for catching butterflies and dragonflies, your net should be made of soft but strong material, with a fine mesh that will not damage the wings of the most delicate insect. Nets come in different shapes and sizes, some with a strong frame for sweeping vegetation and causing insects to fall in.

SMALL CONTAINERS

These are handy for transporting and studying the insects you have captured.

MAGNIFYING GLASS

A small lens, with 10× magnification, as shown here, will give you a more detailed view of the insects you have caught.

INDEX

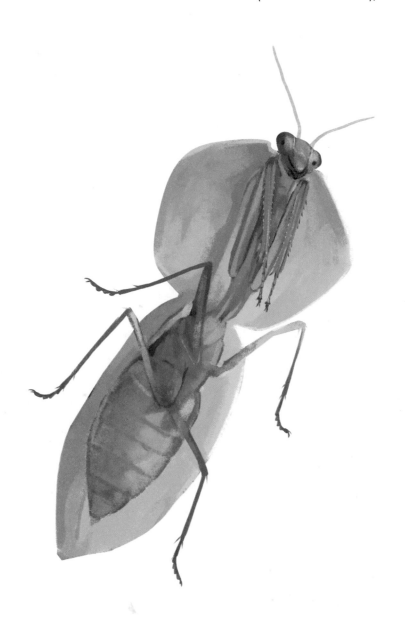

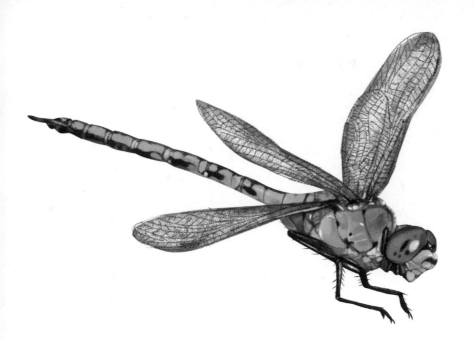

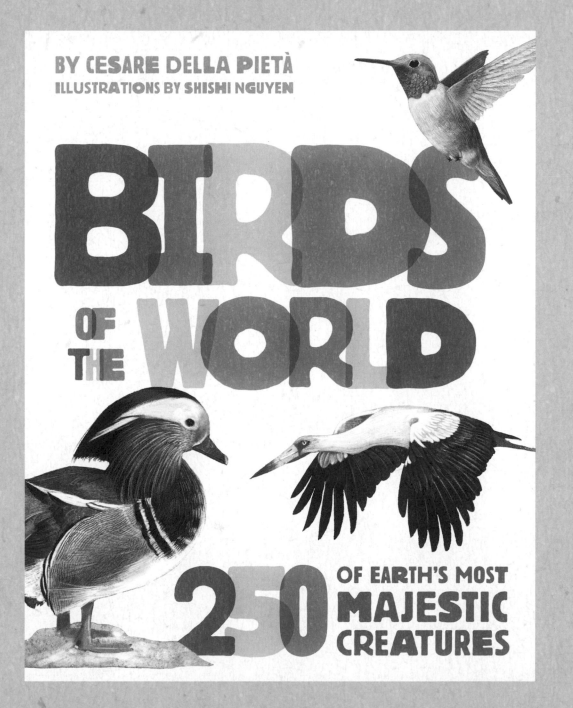

Francesco Tomasinelli was born in Genoa in 1971 and has been fascinated by weird and wonderful animals since he was a child. He began with dinosaurs at the age of three and has never lost interest. After graduating with a degree in marine environmental sciences, he worked for major aquariums in Italy and the United States before devoting himself to publishing, popularizing science, and advising companies and consultancy firms on environmental matters. As a photojournalist, he works with book and magazine publishers in the science and tourism sectors, and with photographic agencies in Italy and the United States. He is the author of the illustrated books *Vado a vivere in città* (*I'm Going to Live in Town*, on urban wildlife), *Oro verde* (*Green Gold*), and *Predatori del microcosmo, le strategia di sopravvivenza di rettili, anfibi, insetti e ragni* (*Predators of the Microcosmos: The Survival Strategies of Reptiles, Amphibians, Insects, and Spiders*) and has contributed images and text to many others. He is a frequent guest on an Italian television geography program and has curated scientific exhibitions for several Italian museums, including *Predatori del Microcosmo* (*Predators of the Microcosmos*), *Piante Guerriere* (*Warrior Plants*), *Alieni* (*Aliens*), and *Kryptòs, mimetismo e inganno in natura* (*Kryptòs: Mimicry and Deception in Nature*). His website is www.isopoda.net.

Yumenokaori is a Vietnamese artist, illustrator, and designer who graduated from the Ho Chi Minh University of Architecture and has published his work in major magazines in various countries. He specializes in wildlife subjects.